THE WELFARE BIND

THE WELFARE BIND

Naomi Gottlieb

Columbia University Press
New York and London   1974

Library of Congress Cataloging in Publication Data

Gottlieb, Naomi, 1925—
    The welfare bind.

    1.   Public welfare—United States.   2.   Public welfare
administration—United States.   I.   Title.
HV95.G66   362.5'0973   73–17259
ISBN 0–231–03762–7

FOR DAVID

Foreword

One of the more propitious offspring of the generally unsuccessful War on Poverty in the 1960s was the welfare rights movement. Few groups are more despised and vilified in our land than welfare recipients; they are widely perceived (even by many of themselves) as laggards who are not to be trusted. Welfare rights organizations, which tended to promise more than their meager resources could deliver, nevertheless provided for many welfare recipients their first opportunity to see and to publicly present themselves as proud, self-respecting, rights-bearing citizens. To observe first hand the effects of such experiences on socially humiliated persons is to witness the birth of hope and confidence, sometimes in sudden, dramatic form.

The significance of the welfare rights movement has been the subject of much dispute. Some have regarded these organizations as the best hope for a radical reordering of the public welfare system. Others maintain that the effects of these organizations on the welfare system are slight and short lived at best. The evidence, if anything, would appear to support the more pessimistic view. The typical welfare rights organization faces enormous obstacles. For one thing, turnover of membership is constant and frequent, a reflection of the constant and frequent turnover among recipients in public welfare agencies. Second, welfare rights organizations typically lack the staff, money, and technical skills needed to effectively organize and execute their programs. Third, expansion of their membership is restricted by the fact that many recipients do not share the aims of the welfare rights movement. And finally, as if all that were not enough, their adversary, the public welfare system, is well insulated by its immense size and complex bureaucratic labyrinths against efforts to reform it.

While the welfare rights movement has not generated the radical reorganization of the public welfare system that some prophesied, neither has it suffered the death others expected. Nationally, and in many communities, welfare rights organizations continue to be a visible force for welfare reform and for advocacy of the rights of recipients. But one important question remains for those concerned more with outcomes than with intentions and promises: exactly what effect have welfare rights organizations had on the behavior of public welfare agencies? It is this question that Dr. Gottlieb has studied and upon which she reports in this book.

In this first systematic study of the subject, Dr. Gottlieb describes in careful detail the interactions between the welfare rights organizations (there were more than one in the community she studied) and the public welfare agency in one large city. She traces in comparable detail the effects of these interactions within the agency. The findings are fascinating and useful. Dr. Gottlieb's research indicates, among other things, that the public welfare agency may be more susceptible to change than was previously believed, particularly if its special vulnerabilities are understood and exploited. Even the efforts by the agency to protect itself against attack from welfare rights organizations sometimes generated, in unexpected ways, changes that were beneficial for recipients.

Dr. Gottlieb is properly cautious about the tentative and limited generality of her findings and conclusions. This is an exploratory study, not designed to generate rigorous proof; but given our ignorance about the subject a more rigorous design would have been infeasible. Dr. Gottlieb's approach is a model for studies of this sort, a model that one hopes will be emulated. The analysis remains close to observable data which are reported in sufficient detail for replication and verification by other observers in other places. Facile inferences and speculation that could be neither confirmed nor refuted are gratefully avoided. Consequently, Dr. Gottlieb's research provides a solid, empirical base for subsequent studies in this area.

Finally, Dr. Gottlieb's research carries a significance beyond the subject of welfare rights organizations. Persons concerned with the fields of social work and social welfare have come to realize that much of what needs to be done involves, in one way or another, bringing about change in social welfare organizations, sometimes quite large and intransigent organizations. With that realization has come the unhappy recognition that we know very little about how organizations change and can be changed. The need is great to develop this knowledge. Dr. Gottlieb's study makes an important contribution to it. It is to be hoped that the obvious value of the research reported here will inspire others to the study of organizational change, and that the excellence of her work will set a standard for subsequent studies in this field.

SCOTT BRIAR
Seattle, Washington

Acknowledgments

Ideas and motivations for a study come from many sources, but there are always key people who spur one's thoughts and research activities. I have been fortunate in the key people associated with this study.

Scott Briar has been a concerned participant throughout this study's considerations, from its earliest beginnings to the latest revisions on the final manuscript. His deep interest in and knowledge about problems of public welfare policy and in the value of social research toward their solution have afforded challenging ideas and most helpful direction. His contribution has been a most happy combination of exciting intellectual consultation and generous encouragement.

From Kermit Wiltse's long-term association with the public welfare field have come many very useful insights into this institution's particular nature. He responded with interest and openness to new ideas related to welfare rights activities and from his considerable experience commented fruitfully on these developments.

Sheldon Messinger's involvement was a keen one, especially at turning points in the study's evolution. He showed an impressive facility for using his considerable knowledge of social institutions for ready translation to the public welfare instance. His observations improved the study at many points.

I am indebted to Barney Glaser and to the members of his seminar in the early months of 1970 for the time and energy they each expended as the utility and creativity of the grounded-theory method of data analysis was demonstrated in developing the basic framework for the study's findings.

Recent critical comments on a final draft by my colleagues Rino Patti and Herman Resnick added yet further clarity. Their insights and support—both given generously—and their convictions about organizational change have improved the final product.

My acknowledgment to the staff of the agency I studied is directly related to the findings. Much of the book is testimony to the harassed conditions under which welfare staff must work, and so my appreciation to them for the time and effort they gave to this research is understandably great.

A NOTE ON PRONOUNS

Lacking less cumbersome forms of pronouns than "his/her" or "himself/herself" to indicate that both men and women are represented in groups of people discussed in the book, I will follow this plan: since both men and women are on the staffs of public welfare agencies, I will alternate the use of the masculine and feminine pronouns when referring to welfare personnel. Since the group of recipients focused on here—members of welfare rights organizations—is almost exclusively women, the feminine pronoun will be employed for them.

Contents

THE WELFARE BIND

CHAPTER ONE

Introduction

This book about humanizing people-serving organizations uses the example of one such organization—the welfare system. There, as is true elsewhere, the staff is enmeshed in an institutional system; the institution itself reflects its role in society; and the result is that the humanity and individuality of the persons served somehow become minimized. The challenges now being made to social institutions question this stifling of individuality, self-respect, and personal integrity.

When local communities insist that medical services seem to be oblivious to their life situations, when parents charge that schools have ignored important aspects of their children's lives, when students claim that the university is an unyielding "knowledge factory," when welfare recipients charge that welfare departments run roughshod over their civil rights, all are demanding that the institutions established to serve them be humanized.

On the face of it, the humanization of social institutions would seem to be a straightforward enough process. You humanize another person when you treat him as an individual and acknowledge his self-respect and inherent dignity. You humanize him when you assume he is an autonomous individual with a right to personal growth; when you recognize the compelling qualities of his life situation; when you believe in his right to choose the services he wishes and to expect that the professional serving him will have his interest uppermost. It is on the basis of these imperatives that challenges have been made to such organizations.

Within most institutional frameworks, meeting these demands is no small task. It may require seeing clients in a new light—with more dignity and autonomy accorded them and with profound changes in traditional relationships between professional and client. It may require being more accountable to clients than to the organization. This forces some disturbing insights into the less obvious purposes of the organization—latent aims that do not appear in any official manual—and into those societal and institutional constraints which have precluded accountability to clients. It requires finding ways—with full awareness of organizational limitations—to be more responsive to client needs.

Enhancing the humanity of clients—acknowledging their self-respect, autonomy, and individual needs in view of typically heavy organizational odds against such acknowledgment —does not come easy for the staff of people-serving institutions. It is difficult to be aware of one's dehumanizing practices, more difficult still to act on that awareness. But there is a payoff. Whatever humanizes clients has the fortunate facility of humanizing staff as well.

PURPOSE OF THE BOOK

This book affords a careful look at one example of the spreading contemporary phenomenon of demands made by clients on the institutions established to serve them. From an understanding of the resultant process of interaction of client and professional, I believe one may see some ways out for both.

Welfare rights organizations—organized groups of welfare recipients—challenge the public welfare system in many ways:

to meet their material needs more adequately, to treat them with respect and dignity, to recognize their legal rights. They assert the right to transform their social status vis-à-vis the institution and demand a say about the circumstances of their lives as recipients. In sum, they demand to be treated as full citizens, autonomous and expecting accountability by the system.

Such challenges throw into relief institutional forces that ordinarily work against humanization of recipients; in the case of welfare the inadequate grants, the accountability upward through the system rather than downward to the clients, the violations of civil rights. The challenges also illuminate staff dilemmas in trying to meet both client and institutional needs. From those client challenges a social process ensues that is related to organizational constraints and to staff's reactions to both the constraints and the demands. A description of that process forms the core of this book. It is hoped that public welfare staff can gain a fuller conceptual grasp of the forces involved in the interplay of client needs and institutional constraints in which they, as professionals, are enmeshed.

However that comprehension by staff is only one part—although an important one—in the potential utility of this study. The interactions described here will lead to some conjectures about possible institutional change toward the client's perspective. Though specific change strategies are suggested, perhaps a more telling outcome is the notion of the potential of transformation from below. Later discussion will make clear the realistic place of staff activities in the whole complex of imperatives of change needed in the welfare structure, but organized recipients do demonstrate that both the impetus and ideas for change can come from below.

The ideas presented here are also addressed to those in social work who are concerned about their profession's stance on public welfare issues. As the public welfare worker may show a greater sense of accountability to her agency than to her client, so the profession as a whole may be charged with a greater commitment to the institutional superstructure than to welfare clientele as a group. The direction of this commitment has been rationalized in the name of professionalism in a narrow sense.

Further, the ideas presented here may be found applicable to humanization efforts at other institutions. The nature of the institution, particularly its latent purpose, has much to do with staff-client interaction, and that will vary with the particular institution. However, the influence of that latent purpose on the interactional process with challenging clients and the idea of change from below may have wider utility and contribute to organizational theory concerning change.

The core of the book, then, is the process of interaction between welfare rights groups and the welfare recipients, as recipients challenge the institution. This forms the basis for subsequent consideration of broader issues of professionalism and humanization, and of change strategies.

BACKGROUND TO THE STUDY

The study was meant to describe what happens within the welfare system when organized recipients make their demands. The questions that guided the study were broadly posed: What effects do welfare rights organizations have on the welfare system? How do they achieve these effects? Those immediately concerned (public welfare personnel and welfare rights members, as well as others adjacent to their interaction—legal-services staff, other community action groups, social agencies) would want to know the effects of welfare rights activities. Further, welfare rights groups reflect the general concern for the prospects of greater responsiveness of social institutions to the needs of those they purport to serve, and the study questions were designed to see if client activities increase this responsiveness.

The focus was on the interaction between welfare rights groups and the welfare agency rather than on specific outcomes of recipient activities. I have assumed that there would be a range of responses by welfare personnel to the pressures of welfare rights groups and that these responses would in turn lead to altered activities by the recipient groups.

The other intent of this inquiry was to understand this interactive process as primarily an agency phenomenon. Given the interest in the potential for enhanced agency responsiveness as a result of recipient actions, it was logical to look at the behavior and attitudes of agency staff. If the welfare system remains impervious to the demands of recipients, or if it shifts some of its policies and procedures as a consequence, the accounting of either of these eventualities lies to a great extent within the agency. Answers might be found in the structural features of the welfare system, in the conditions of the staff's work lives, and in circumstances (including broader societal attitudes) that preclude or enhance a more humanistic response to clients.

This focus on the agency staff is not meant to minimize what the welfare rights groups themselves bring to the situation; the strategies they evolve and the viability of their organizations contribute in a major way. However the staff's response may give a more immediate answer to the questions of how the humanization of this social institution may be effected. Whatever the client pressures, whether the agency stands stock still or bends at all depends to a large extent on the staff's response. In addition, it is my conviction that too much emphasis has been given to studying the poor in interaction with welfare institutions. Half of that interaction comes from the office side of the desk and social workers need to examine their own contributions.

The study's purpose then was to describe the interaction between welfare rights organizations and the welfare system, and to see this process through an understanding of the welfare staff's perspective. The data were collected in a public welfare department in an urban center, primarily in the AFDC (Aid to Families With Dependent Children) division. In this city and nationally, AFDC recipients predominate as welfare rights members and AFDC divisions are the prime target of their activities.

Two techniques were used to understand welfare rights interactions through the staff's eyes: the first was to interview the staff members about their welfare rights experiences, some individually but most in groups of workers and their supervisors; the second was to observe a series of meetings at all levels of the welfare system. These meetings included deliberations of welfare issues by the city's governing bodies, meetings of the policymaking commission for the welfare department, public hearings called by the state department of welfare, and intra-agency meetings at various administrative levels. The methodological appendix describes the research process more fully, but essentially the objective of data-gathering was a description of the usual work pressures of the staff as the context in which welfare rights interactions could be better understood.

The welfare department studied is, like all such agencies, set both within the welfare system network and within other parts of the city's governing structure. It is in a state whose counties are separately responsible for the provision of welfare services, but answerable in certain respects to the state's administrative offices. Each of these units—state and local—must, in turn, meet certain Federal standards. Bounded by these state and Federal structures, policy for the welfare department is made by a five-member welfare commission, appointed by the city's mayor and answerable on such selected issues as finances to the city's governing board, an elected body. Working committees of that body, such as the finance commission, play a crucial role in department matters.

During the time of the study, welfare rights groups appeared in interaction with all levels of this welfare structure. At the welfare department offices they acted as advocates for their members in individual complaints, came as group delegations on issues affecting many clients, and engaged in organizing activities (e.g., gave out leaflets in the waiting rooms). They regularly attended the biweekly meetings of the policymaking welfare commission, and they often appeared at the meetings of the city's governing boards and their working committees. When recipients appealed the actions of the local agency to the state department of welfare, welfare rights members acted as representatives and advocates for their members.

There is no way to know whether this agency is typical of welfare departments in a general sense and in its relations with recipient groups. It was chosen because it was in an urban center in which there were fairly numerous and active welfare rights groups. Because only one city was involved and because this was an exploratory inquiry using open methods of interviewing and observation, the findings are not presented as verified and generalizable, but in the form of a set of tentative but hopefully plausible, internally consistent ideas, derived from the data. The applicability to other situations can only become known if some of the ideas suggested here are tested for fit or modification elsewhere. For, in essence, this will be a series of hypotheses about the interactional process between recipient organizations and the welfare system.

BASIC ELEMENTS OF THE WELFARE-RIGHTS— WELFARE-SYSTEM INTERACTION

The existence of what is termed "the bind" is a major condition of the welfare system. The bind, experienced by welfare staff, is the consequence of the disparity between the needs of clients and administrative restrictions on their fulfillment; it also results from the conflicting charge to staff both to investigate and to rehabilitate. The disparity and the contradictory charge have a continuing and inherently stressful effect on staff. The significance of the bind is attested to by several sources: (1) sociological analyses revealing the ambiguous nature of attitudes toward the assisted poor; (2) programs based on these societal views, which place welfare staff in an untenable position; (3) the universality of its effects on personnel throughout the welfare system. The bind is not a static entity in this analysis. Its nature and extent is affected by other elements in the situation; for example, the manner in which staff adheres to rules can soften or sharpen the effects of the bind.

Extensive and proliferating rules reflect the contradictions of the system which create the bind; they are the focal point of welfare rights demands. Like the bind, the rules are not static, but are constantly changing in construction and interpretation. Though they would seem a force controlling clients and workers impersonally and equally, rules, in fact, vary both in adherence and enforceability and are used variously by staff in their adaptations to the bind.

As organizations of those previously unorganized, welfare rights groups challenge the system in new ways. They insist on the legitimacy of their demands (based on rules), alter the bind by becoming vocal participants and no longer permit rule interpretations by agents of the system alone.

The response of agency personnel to welfare rights demands appears to be related to three interlocking factors: managing the bind, appraising the demands, manipulating the rules. The kinds of response may usefully be differentiated as either disruptive or nondisruptive for usual agency operations. This distinction has two purposes: to see the ways in which staff members soften the impact of demands to keep the bind manageable, and to see if some statement can be made concerning which demands about which rules lead to disruptive responses. The latter bears on prospects for change in the system via welfare rights actions. There are also largely unexpected findings of multipurpose functions which welfare rights groups serve for the staff.

The focus is on the process itself—as a description and explanation of staff behavior in interaction with organized recipients. The elements in this analytic description—the bind, the rules, the demands, the responses—would be present in other welfare situations and therefore this discussion has the potential for wider social welfare applicability. With some modification, the model for analysis may also be generalized to other circumstances in which organized clients challenge service institutions.

There is literature on the influence of organizational purpose,[1] on manifest and latent functions of organizations [2] and on the effects on social workers of agency restrictions.[3] There is not a sufficiently clear statement, however, about the existence of contradictory charges to staff and of the blatant contrast between rhetoric and practice. There is literature on the broad subject of social movement and protest [4] and on the phenomenon of citizen participation in poverty programs.[5] There was an opportunity here, however, to focus more directly on the interaction between professionals and clients as a social movement meets an established institution—one with a special potential for conflict—head on.

My study deals with demands for rights and new relationships and with the changes in agency behavior as a consequence of these assertions. It will be a peculiar mixture of contemporary protests and centuries-old prejudices. Though welfare rights groups developed nationally and in the city under study at a time of burgeoning organizations of the disadvantaged and in the era of the slogan "maximum feasible participation of the poor," societal attitudes toward welfare recipients remain ponderous and determinative. The outcome of pressures that welfare rights organizations bring to bear on the welfare agency are determined as much, or more, by old and persistent attitudes toward the assisted poor as by current notions of their political participation. Though the welfare system is an institution established ostensibly for the benefit of welfare recipients, there is much evidence for the view that this system has "contempt for its beneficiaries" [6] and that the latent purpose is to derogate recipients.

RACISM AND THE WELFARE SYSTEM

Black and other nonwhite people are overrepresented among the poor and among welfare recipients. Though whites are still by far the majority of low-income persons—both among those groups receiving public assistance and those not receiving it—the number of impoverished nonwhites is far out of proportion to their numbers within the general population. In a vicious circle, racism helps to create the problems leading to poverty and welfare dependency, as the Kerner report so impressively documented,[7] and then racism operates to rationalize public derogation of the recipient. The societal forces underlying harsh public attitudes toward recipients are compounded for nonwhite people because of racism, and in fact for many people the symbol of the welfare recipient is the black person, particularly the black mother. That symbol, used to derogate, remains impervious to the facts about who is a typical recipient. The repressive 1967 Social Security Amendments were claimed to be a racist reaction to the tremendous increase in numbers of urban recipients, many of whom were nonwhite. Further, the public welfare institution itself is not immune from the racism that affects society as a whole. The Kerner report contains, in its recommendations for national actions, a separate section for public welfare. The leaders and many of the members of the welfare rights movement are black, so the issue of racism may again be a determinant in institutional responses. Thus, the interrelationship between race and the welfare problem cannot be overestimated.

I stress the client-professional dichotomy rather than the chasm between people created by racist attitudes in my search for factors to describe and help explain the interaction of professionals and clients, as clients protested agency practices.

Granted the existence of racism throughout all social institutions, this emphasis on determinants that go beyond the issue
of race and apply to whites as well nevertheless seems to hold
promise for wider applicability. As a result there was no attempt to look carefully at how a person's racial attitudes might
affect the welfare rights staff interaction (there were white and
nonwhite participants on both sides of these interchanges), and
no systematic appraisal of how practices were specifically applied to nonwhite recipients or by nonwhite staff. Because of
racism, the effects of the system as described here will be compounded for the nonwhite participant. Other students of this
phenomenon may later find that including the impact of racism will add in important ways to the process of interaction
presented here.

THE BOOK'S FORMAT AND
PROSPECTS FOR HUMANIZATION

My analysis of welfare-rights–welfare-system interaction will be
in the form of a series of tentative explanations. This will
relate to the implications of the bind in which contradictions
place staff, the place of rules in reflecting organizational goals
and in bolstering recipients' demands, and the assessment of
and response to these demands by agency staff. The presentation can be seen in two lights, distinct but related. The description specifies what happens when welfare rights organizations prod the welfare system, and that portrait may be a
significant contribution in and of itself to an understanding of
client input to organizational life. The phenomenon of a recipient organization, new to this generation, has not been seen
since the Depression years.

An analytic view of this process of interaction can have a further impact, however, perhaps of far more consequence to the
overriding concern for increased humanization. Welfare rights
challenges act as a prism, forcing into an uncomfortable glare
aspects of the welfare system that would otherwise remain

murky. The organized recipient demands that the welfare staff be answerable to her—her needs and rights—and so the issue of accountability is illuminated. Similarly exposed is the bind —a result, in part, of a crossfire of obligations. One is led to question the usual direction of the staff's commitment and to wonder if the mantle of professionalism has been illused. Recipient activities also clarify the contradictions in the system which make it so vulnerable to challenges from below, and by refusing traditional agency-client relationships the recipient makes the dehumanizing practices of the agency more explicit. Such issues as these—accountability, vulnerability, dehumanization —are magnified for clearer perception because of welfare rights challenges.

Clearer also are ideas for change that can be gleaned from an understanding of the process. It is from the organized recipient's stance per se that the notion of change from below is suggested. It is from observed responses of the welfare staff that possible planned strategies come to mind. As a prologue to wider issues this leads to some theoretical concerns relevant to humanization and to some change strategies for its greater realization.

CHAPTER TWO

The Welfare System Bind

A perspective somewhat different from that usually found in the literature is needed to establish the nature of the bind for welfare staff. A perusal of public welfare writings reveals two broad kinds of commentaries: the first is a focus on the administration of public assistance with analysis of how both assistance and services might be improved,[1] including critiques of social services; [2] the second is the recipient's view, primarily an accounting of the abuses of the system.[3] Neither sort of discussion takes into account that practices which dehumanize the recipient also severely affect the staff. Society has some distinct attitudes toward the assisted poor and the people hired to express those attitudes through assistance programs are placed in a seriously contradictory position.

It may seem at times in this report that the staff members are the ones affected most by the welfare system. Obviously, this is not the case. The welfare institution is the staff's working life; for the recipient it can be her whole life. The recipient remains in poverty; the staff receives a comfortable salary. The report is oriented to the staff for reasons discussed earlier, but the disparity of the system's effects on these two groups is in no way forgotten.

SOURCES OF THE BIND

The persistence of views about granting public money to those in poverty is impressive. Residues of the Poor Laws of the seventeenth century continue to influence current programs. Perhaps the most telling remnant of all is that a person's need for aid is her own fault and that recipient status is a personal disgrace.[4] Despite official statements about the right of people to receive public assistance, there is overwhelming evidence from all sides—the press, governmental debates, scholarly studies—that the stigma attached to the welfare check is almost as tangible as the paper it is written on. One would be hard put to quarrel with Sarbin's categorization of welfare recipients as nonpersons—those with a degraded social identity.[5] Yet societal views on public aid remain ambivalent. We spend a great deal of money on public assistance ($10.6 billion in fiscal 1971–72) but it is an "ill-given dole."[6] By and large, the public does not become aroused about the numbers of people who live in dire poverty but who use their own funds. It becomes indignant to the point of fury, at times, about the numbers of people who must be aided from public monies. One wonders about the deep wellspring of such strong societal convictions. Consider these statements:

Simmel

Assistance to which the community is committed in its own interest, but which the poor person . . . has no right to claim, makes the poor person into an object of the activity of the group and places him at a distance from the whole, which at times makes him live as a "corpus vile" by the mercy of the whole at times, and because of this, makes him into its bitterest enemy.[7]

A welfare recipient

I kept hoping somehow we wouldn't have to go. You should work for what you get. It seemed wrong to go. This is meant

for slum people. I would not have applied at all if it weren't
for a physical injury. I would have starved first.[8]

An impoverished tenant farmer

They're all leeches, those people who go down there and get
help. If they can't help themselves, they shouldn't get married.
We don't have enough to eat for our kids a lot of the time, but
I don't want no handouts.[9]

The recipient and the tenant farmer graphically describe the
social phenomenon which Simmel presents in theory. Our society places those who need assistance in such a position that
most people feel that an application for aid is to be avoided at
all costs. Welfare assistance carries neither the connotation of a
right to claim benefits nor anything of the character of a contract. There has been no reciprocal arrangement leading to this
aid, and this lack of reciprocity is offered as one possible explanation of antirecipient feelings.

The strength of this social force is suggested by Gouldner,
who describes the norm of reciprocity as a universal attribute
that exercises great influence on all kinds of personal interactions.[10] Different from behavioral expectations deriving from
an individual's status or his socially standardized role, reciprocity implies both rights and obligations based on past actions—
"we owe others certain things because of what they have previously done for us." [11]

The sources for the norm of reciprocity lie buried in the
history of the earliest social interchanges, but conjectures about
its origins have been made by Mauss in his studies of primitive
societies. Members of these societies believe that

> to receive something is to receive part of someone's spiritual es-
> sence. To keep this thing is dangerous, not only because it is il-
> licit to do so, but also because it comes morally, physically and
> spiritually from another person. . . . The gift is thus something
> that must be given, that must be received and that is, at the
> same time, dangerous to accept.[12]

The dangerous primitive spirit in the gift may have been transmuted over time into the present danger of dependence which is only dispelled by reciprocation. Interestingly, Mauss cites another society in which the word "gift" has two meanings —that of gift and that of poison.

Thus, the norm of reciprocity is a universal social attribute, is based on what people have done for each other in the past or will do in the future, and has attached to it certain perils. Gouldner suggests that there are certain circumstances in which the norm of reciprocity may be, in a sense, suspended. Society makes allowances in these circumstances, and it is from these allowances as well as the norm itself that we can see gradations in society's attitudes toward those who receive public aid. The aged and disabled may be exempt, but not so the able-bodied person who has made no contribution in a reciprocal arrangement, as has a neighbor who receives unemployment compensation or Social Security benefits. This recipient gets the full force of the kind of condemnation contained in a letter to the *New York Times* after the Newburgh episode of 1961 in which the writer wondered why "those receiving unearned benefits from the public purse should not suffer the social stigma that is rightfully theirs." [13]

Added to the anger society feels toward the person who has not and probably will not reciprocate are the less than humanitarian reasons prompting society's offer of aid. Simmel suggests that aid is proferred

> so that the poor will not become active and dangerous enemies of the state . . . for if assistance were to be based on the interests of the poor person there would, in principle, be no limit whatsoever on the transmission of property in favor of the poor.[14]

Following this argument and relating it to reciprocity, it can be seen that both partners in this relationship are in conflict. The recipient feels he should have reciprocated and yet sees no way to do this. The donor in a sense feels he is meeting more than his end of the bargain and yet knows too that the recipient himself is not the end of his welfare activity. Conot describes this phenomenon from the point of view of a black man in Watts: "In due time, he learned that the nation, while considering him a bum, would, with its social conscience, not let his wife and children starve." [15] In a sense, then, both the recipient and the donor-society are in an anomalous position.

To add another dimension to the description of the relationship between recipient and society and to explain the morally reprehensible connotation of welfare, there is Beck's consideration of welfare as a "moral category." The workings of the norm of reciprocity can be encompassed in Beck's view of society vis-à-vis the recipient.

Beck asserts there is a folk theory of the structure of society that in effect claims that the accepted way of life works well for everyone: "Any member of a population can be 'injected' into some reasonable place in the institutionalized role structure." That for long periods of time, in many societies, the reality contradicts this picture does not appreciably affect the members' attachment to the ideal. However, society must find a way of accounting for the group of "roleless" people, who are "in the population but outside the positions and careers specified by the Theory." This explanation must not, of course, violate the belief in the efficacy of the system, and it may be that it is a genuine adherence to that theory, rather than any conscious attempt to hide its flaws, that leads to some "logical" explanation of this outside group. The discrepancy is handily explained by the

> motivations and character of the people found within the residual category . . . by lack of motivation, or moral strength and the like . . . [they] have defaulted on the system rather than being the victims of an inadequately articulated system.

What is thereby avoided is a "public scandal to the Structure." [16] The incongruity of job training centers (for work motivation as well as skills) in the light of increasing levels of unemployment seems to suggest the necessity of avoiding such a scandal.[17] Ryan's persuasive argument that we consistently "blame the victim" of society's failures and inequities both confirms Beck's position and indicates that the welfare case is only one among many.

Whatever factors may be called upon to explain the societal definition of the recipient's status, there is little question of the depth of the public's reaction. It may be all too obvious to mention that this is hardly a question of amounts of monies involved. One need only compare welfare costs with other public expenditures, such as the military or subsidies of various sorts, to be aware of this. But consider the feeling reflected in the following statements.

Senator Russell Long (Democrat of Louisiana), at hearings concerning work training programs for mothers of young children

> With regard to unemployment insurance, we talk about something a person has earned. . . . I just hope we never get to the point where everybody has a right—able-bodied people have the right—to expect welfare payments though they decline to work. It seems to me that the right to go hungry, if you don't want to work, should be preserved in this country.[18]

Gary Allen in American Opinion

> The War on Poverty is really a war on property based on forcibly extracting money from citizens who earned it, and giving it to those who have not earned it. . . . Any government predicated upon robbing its industrious citizens to support the indolent and corrupt *must* ultimately collapse as the producers are eventually engulfed by the parasites.[19]

Commissioner Plogh, San Antonio City Council

> Why should the public help those families (of malnourished children)? . . . The trouble is all because some men just ain't worth a dime.[20]

These are extreme statements representing politically conservative views. Most Americans might not speak so forcefully about welfare recipients but I believe they would speak in somewhat the same vein. Most people believe that recipients should make it on their own and that to be a recipient is to be degraded. What is additionally significant is that by and large, recipients incorporate these attitudes toward themselves, leading to what Nonet has termed "moral captivity"—an acceptance of the terms and consequences of others' definition of one as appropriately divested of certain status and rights.[21] Perhaps the most noteworthy aspect of the welfare rights phenomenon is the recipients' rejection of that stance.

PROGRAM COMPONENTS OF THE BIND

The broad effects of these antiwelfare opinions are several, and as each is noted there begins a specific cataloging of the components of the bind on staff.

First of all, little money is given to recipients and what is given reflects the deserving and undeserving distinction. Need as established by individual states (Federal standards relate largely to procedure and not to adequacy of grants) is well below the poverty line, and in 34 states AFDC payments are less than 100 percent of that need. In seven states, in fact, grants are less than 50 percent of that basic level. An average monthly payment to a member of an AFDC family is $52.75, considerably less than the $77.92 paid to someone receiving Old Age Assistance.[22] In the welfare department studied here the amount received by a family of four was then $282.00. An important element of the bind, then, is that no matter how compassionately or efficiently the social worker does her job, her client will not have enough money to buy the barest necessities.

Evolving from the view of recipiency status as an individual rather than a social phenomenon is a whole configuration of policies and programs aimed at individual rehabilitation rather than social change. As a point of contrast, Glazer notes that national assistance in England is

> viewed, at least officially, as an adaptation to some bad fitting planks in the national [welfare] floor, rather than a sign of failure or inadequacy and moral defect as it is here.[23]

Here, however, programs such as that embodied in the 1962 Services Amendments to the Social Security Act declared that welfare recipients needed individual rehabilitation in addition to money. Implications of this approach are multiple: 1) that the individual's future prospects for independence depend on her particular situation; 2) that self-sufficiency is not primarily a question of the availability of jobs or child care services; 3) that the amount of the grant is almost irrelevant if personal problems can be addressed.[24]

Social work as a profession has been an integral part of this individual emphasis.[25] Social workers can, with firm professional backing, assign a diagnosis of psychopathic personality or character disorder to a welfare recipient. They may fail to see that, insofar as social attitudes about the focus of blame for the dependency are concerned, there is only a fine line of distinction between that kind of personal assessment and the layman's view of the recipient as morally degraded. In each instance, society's finger is pointed in the same direction.

In addition, along with the stigma attached to the check has come compulsory casework services. The current shift to the separation of services and eligibility does give the client more freedom about the receipt of services, but this change in itself does not dilute the emphasis on the individual as the locus of the problem. Also, as part of the professional equipment for dealing with recipient problems is a set of ideas about lower-class life, particularly nonwhite lower-class life, which is beginning to receive much-needed challenge.[26]

The irony of the caseworker's role in the public welfare situation is that in actual practice in most welfare departments, and certainly in the one under study, there is virtually no time for services. Even when the amount of time and the number of trained workers is sufficient, the results are at best problematic [27] and their effectiveness in decreasing dependency has never been documented.[28] It is clear however that social work's posture has contributed to the notion of the primacy of individual responsibility for recipiency status.

There are certainly individuals whose particular personal problems add to or cause their economic dependency and who might benefit from professional services. This of course is not the issue here, nor is the increased awareness of the extent of poverty. We are a long way from Galbraith's analysis of "case" and "insular" poverty,[29] and there is general recognition that when one-fifth of the nation lives in poverty, there is a national problem of considerable proportions. What is of interest to this discussion is that basic efforts to eliminate poverty—something by way of a guaranteed income for all the poor—comes up against the kind of attitudes toward the assisted poor already mentioned. The many discussions of a guaranteed income [30] treat the comparative advantages of different methods—the costs, the coverage, the effectiveness, etc.—but when the subject of possible adoption is approached, then we are in the area of what is possible politically; and that means public attitudes toward the poor.

Certain consequences of these attitudes have been cited as part of the bind: the very inadequate grants and the designation of the individual as the cause of his dependency. There is also a packet of procedures to which the recipient must conform and which the social worker must administer, deriving again from societal doubts about the character of recipients and the need to control carefully the eligibility and continued dependency of each recipient. These procedures have only recently been challenged on their legality. The development of a separate field of welfare law [31] and the mushrooming of legal services for the poor have brought to public attention a number of violations of basic rights of recipients.

The result has been a delineation of those procedures, not

only of questionable legality, but also illustrative of society's distinctive stance toward recipients.

"The ills" Handler writes,

> come about in two ways. First, there is bad substantive legislation. . . . Second, there are broad delegations of authority to welfare agencies which allow them to define critical substantive matters.[32]

The consequences may best be noted by some brief extracts from legal commentaries on the nature of procedures and the position of recipients vis-à-vis the illegalities.

Lawyers have made specific attacks on the illegalities of welfare policies.

> Day to day administration has resulted in many instances of plainly lawless administrative behavior: that is, administrative officials are acting contrary to the Constitution and/or statutory terms and clients are deprived of rights embodied in constitutional and statutory law.[33]

> No more insidious invasion of the rights of welfare subjects exists than the ubiquitous tendency to impose upon the welfare recipient standards of morality which are a matter of free choice for other citizens.[34]

> In no other area of entitlement, such as social security or veteran's benefits, are there similar pressures to impose a moral code.[35]

Lawyers have also made very clear the difficulties that recipients encounter in defending their own rights:

> The recipient has (1) prior contact or experience with the "law" resulting in alienation from the legal process, and (2) a general condition of dependency and insecurity leading to fear of reprisal if legal remedies were to be pursued.[36]

> A major reason [for client's acceptance of midnight searches] is that persons on public assistance are in no position to enforce a

constitutional right of privacy. . . . The only way to bar the searches is to refuse to admit the investigator and . . . that means risking the loss of subsistence for the family.[37]

THE SPECIAL CASE OF AFDC

Recent court decisions on the illegality of the "midnight raid" on AFDC recipients have pointed to perhaps the most dramatic example of the expectations by the system of workers' invasion of clients' privacy, but there are other, less blatant and more extensive, incursions on the lives of recipients. Such controls over recipients are most evident in the AFDC program, for whatever has already been suggested about society and recipiency status is compounded here. AFDC reflects a geometric progression of conflicting feelings toward recipients. In contrast to such programs as those for the disabled and elderly, AFDC is a target for public harassment on the issue of sexual morality, of child neglect, of the indolent, generation-upon-generation welfare family. It is a giant thorn in the side of the welfare establishment, for, in Beck's terms, it is too much of a reminder that something is out of kilter.

The program was almost an afterthought when the Social Security Act was first enacted. Witte points to the marked disinterest in ADC in 1935 to the extent of its being included because no one was concerned enough to argue against it. Further, grants for the child's caretaker were not included until 1950. It took 15 years to acknowledge that a dependent-child case involved a needy adult. In addition, many aspects, such as money payments, fair hearing, Federal standards, included originally for old age assistance were made part of the AFDC program as well only for the sake of uniformity in all programs.[38]

AFDC was supposed to have "withered away" with the rest of public assistance as social insurance went into full gear; but of course, to the exasperation of welfare planners and many others, it has increased multifold. Called the stepchild of the welfare system, AFDC has become an unruly stepchild. It has mushroomed, Steiner contends, because "the present character of the ADC rolls was never included as part of the 'withering away' theory." [39] We are faced then with situations such as that of New York where AFDC caseloads increased by 40 percent from 1953 to 1967.[40] Today, fathers absent by separation or desertion, rather than by death or disability, account for an overwhelming portion of the AFDC population. This is a major shift over the past twenty years.[41] The situation reflects such problems as undereducation and underemployment, and is to a great extent a harsh reminder of the unresolved problem of race.[42]

It is an irony of the present situation that the consequences of precisely those social dysfunctions which cause the burgeoning AFDC lists—the inability of our society to use constructively the hard-to-employ, particularly the nonwhite—are used to derogate the affected group. Superimposed on these labels are a host of social problems assigned to recipients—alcoholism, juvenile delinquency, illegitimacy, child neglect, mental illness—which are reputed to be rampant in the AFDC population. Such notions remain impervious to careful studies which document their mythlike qualities.[43] Also impervious are the problems which lead to the economic dependency.

As a consequence of the stubborn caseloads and social attitudes, procedures evolve which are responsive to public opinion but which, in turn, have at the least ironic, and at the most destructive, effects, and which do little to lighten the welfare burden. The NOLEO requirement—that local law enforcement officials be notified as AFDC desertion cases are activated to force support from fathers—was enacted, Cohen says, by Congress, which "in initiating and adopting the amendment was responding to public opinion and at the same time trying to work out something constructive." [44] In actuality

the lack of uniform practice among prosecuting attorneys, the persistent confusion in the function with that of fraud prosecutions, and the general inability of dependent persons to defend themselves in the face of investigation by law enforcement officials have created a multitude of opportunities for discrimination and abusive treatment.[45]

What has remained questionable is that the amount of money realized through these procedures is worth the cost of enforcing them.[46]

Suitable home provisions—for substitute care of the child if the AFDC home is considered inadequate (some states have attempted to designate the second illegitimate birth as reason enough)—permits denial of aid to a mother who does not maintain a "suitable home." The incongruity of this is seen again in the lack of effect on AFDC numbers and in the increased costs involved if a child is placed elsewhere.

The work provisions of the 1967 Social Security Amendments offer yet another example of additions to the administrative superstructure responsive to public opinion with questionable impact on the overall problem.

These few illustrations are not meant as a critique of the welfare system, though they are partly that,[47] but mainly to emphasize the position in which these procedures place the staff. Welfare workers are given broad discretionary powers over the most personal aspects of the lives of recipients, along with expectations of most picayune attention to the accounting of every aspect of financial eligibility. No wonder that the local administration of public welfare has been called "one of the most disheartening works of men." [48]

All that has been said to this point about the welfare system could be summed up in its characterization as a social institution which by its very nature puts people down.[49] Recipiency status is a degraded role in our society and inevitably the agency assigned to determine and control that status must take that basic stance towards its clients. What are the implications of such an essential purpose of this institution? Because society believes that most people, and certainly most of those in the

AFDC program, should not receive aid but should be independent, they must make very sure that only those who are clearly eligible receive aid, and only for so long as is absolutely necessary.[50] The results are involved investigations, all manner of controls, all the ramifications of the means test, and often violations of rights.

THE ROLE OF THE STAFF

The question then becomes: how does one envision the staff's role in all of this? It is possible to see public welfare workers as witting or unwitting agents for middle-class control of the poor, with many of the staff's psychological problems fitting the role of investigators. They can also be seen as professionals who serve in agencies created to help, not exploit, the poor and who, despite bothersome though necessary procedures, use expert social evaluations only to decide what is best for individual families.[51] The stance taken in this study is very well expressed by Grosser and Sparer:

> The violations of the rights of welfare clients do not stem from character defects or malicious intent on the part of welfare officials. Obviously, any large bureaucracy will include workers of varying convictions and competencies. Inadequate salaries, overburdened workloads and thankless tasks result in an unusual turnover within welfare departments but they do not create the basic problem. In part, the problem stems from broader societal attitudes.[52]

The assumption is made here that any public welfare staff consists of persons exhibiting the gamut of psychological makeups, of motivations for working in public welfare, of viewpoints about recipients—some mirroring general opinion and some at great variance from it—and that it would not be possible to characterize staff members as bureaucrats in the pejorative sense of that term or as professionals in the best sense. Further, my stance is that the bind is the basic problem and would continue to be operative no matter the nature of the staff.[53] The point to be emphasized is that the elements of the bind are inherent in the welfare situation. There may be varying levels of consciousness in the staff about its effect (and for some the pull from below may be nonoperative), but there is always the possibility that proclient pressures may surface to create within the staff a more fully sensed dilemma.

To an extent, the bind is a dehumanizing force for all staff. To make this point, I would single out two aspects of an individual's humanity—his empathy and his autonomy—and conjecture as to the way these are affected by the role of public welfare worker. When procedures reflect the kind of societal attitudes discussed above and expectations are for a performance with more of an investigative character than a client-oriented one, conditions for empathy are severely restricted. An effective comparison can be made with another societal agent: It is expected that the prison guard will be more a custodian than rehabilitator and the prison staff finds far less support for its role of therapist than for that of custodian.[54] Though one of the bases of the bind in welfare already noted was the simultaneous charge of investigator and rehabilitator, there seems little question that, as with the prison situation, the public expects the second function to be met, but as subsidiary to and not at the expense of the first. Empathy has a hard time finding its way here. Autonomy is similarly hampered. Bureaucracies dealing with low-income people are the ones most heavily laden with rules, which is tantamount to saying that staff autonomy is singularly limited.

This potentially conflicting and dehumanizing situation exists because staff cannot meet the needs of their clients owing to administrative limitations and because they cannot fulfill simultaneously the investigatory and rehabilitative expectations of the system. For this analysis, the end-result of this combination of factors—the bind on the staff rather than individual predilections or general organizational factors—serves as a backdrop for the behavior of the staff in the agency under study.

Certain assumptions need to be stated to explain how the data were reasonably taken to indicate the existence of this bind.[55] I am not asserting that acute feelings of this vise were overwhelmingly present among most staff members or even that such feelings predominated. I have assumed that whatever conflictual feelings were expressed existed alongside other attitudes. When a worker laments the lack of money for school clothes, other convictions may very well be operating—e.g., many of these mothers should not be receiving welfare at all, they should learn to economize, the children should get part-time jobs, it's their own fault anyway—but to a certain extent that person is aware of the discrepancy between needs and money available and believes that there are many families in which the mother cannot work and in which the children do not have adequate clothing. I have made no effort to measure and weigh the variety of attitudes expressed or the predominance of pro- or antirecipient feeling, but I have assumed that the views expressed about the conflict were part of the person's configuration of feelings. It seemed unreasonable to assume a completely callous stance, or for that matter a complete identification with and empathy for the client. Neither stance would be a reasonable interpretation of the staff's position. What I have assumed is that statements made in interviews, in group discussions with colleagues, and at public meetings are reflective of at least part of those persons' feelings about the recipient's situation and—this is the critical point—that these feelings are the ones tapped by welfare rights prodding. I have concluded from these statements that for most people in welfare there is an awareness, admittedly of varying intensity, of conflict around the unmet needs of clients.

Thus, a member of the city's finance commission says he

knows that people will suffer because the welfare budget will be cut, but there just isn't enough tax revenue to meet the burden. "We don't get the help we need from the state."

The state hearing officer at an appeal procedure tells the recipient that he doesn't know how she can possibly manage on the small grant she receives.

One of the welfare commissioners says that if only the state maximum grant limitation were lifted, needed money could be provided for clients. Another remarked that "we seem to be these people's enemies."

The agency director states that the budget schedule as enforced by state and county does not meet client needs.

Supervisors in divisional meetings state that clients do not have enough to live on and gross family problems are going unattended because of lack of staff time.

Workers complain that both they and their clients have to live with endless, restrictive rules, that recipients do not have sufficient money to feed their families, and that getting out a seriously inadequate check is about all they have time to do for clients. "All I do is say no to my clients."

Variations of the above statements were made at all levels of the system (welfare rights presses all levels) but were more intensely and frequently evident among workers and supervisors —those with closest direct contact with recipients. And for them especially, ordinary work pressures serve to intensify the bind.

THE WORKLOAD AND THE BIND

The staff itself would hardly require further documentation than its own experiences about the oppressive workload in public welfare work. It is documented in many places, however.[56] This agency may have an unusually high turnover rate adding to the usual pressure, but high turnover is characteristic of all of public welfare. Tremendous work pressures were everywhere evident in the agency: in statements made to me and others and in observations. Workers spoke of caseloads of 85 instead of 60 and uncovered caseloads resulting in additional work for both supervisors and workers,[57] of group intake because there wasn't time for individual applications, of a backlog of many hundreds of referrals for work training programs. The word "chaos" was used on a number of occasions to describe the situation and a plea was made in an administrative meeting that the agency acknowledge that workers do not have time to complete the work required. Meetings observed reflected this sense of pressure palpably, as did observations of workers at their desks and in larger meetings. Divisional meetings exhibited a wearying attempt by upper-echelon personnel to meet their own unending demands without adding to the burdens of staff below them. Leaving one of these sessions, a harassed supervisor talked of "going around in endless circles and never getting anywhere."

As a consequence of the kinds of controls the agency imposes, investigatory procedures and paperwork proliferate. The workload adds to the bind in at least several ways: (1) It takes more time to make certain of a recipient's eligibility than it does to deny him aid. The assumption is that denial adds to the conflict about clients' unmet needs.[58] (2) There is often not even enough time for workers to send out the money for which clients are eligible. (3) When there is no time for services, there is also no opportunity for workers to help clients adjust to the inadequacies and so ease the strain for both. (4) A very harried worker is that much more vulnerable to the complaints and demands of recipients. Thus, the procedures comprise part of the bind by structuring the situation so that workers must control recipients, rather than trusting or helping them. In turn, the work involved in completing the procedures limits the opportunities to ease the bind and often increases it.

The frustrated reactions to these conditions shown by many was not universal, however. Staff showed varied responses to the bind.

ADAPTATIONS TO THE BIND

Perhaps the most appropriate introduction to the range of adaptations made to the bind is the acknowledgement that the job would be impossible without some way out. Of course, for many the job does become intolerable, and so one might consider the immense turnover in staff as the most extreme consequence of the bind. For those who remain, the combination of overwork, the nature of agency-client relations, and the doubtful outcome for the clients serviced makes some sort of adaptive mechanism imperative, granted, as is done here, at least a modicum of humane concern for recipients. The choice of accommodations may be a matter of a number of factors not treated here: individual personality, professional training, dominant reference group, political attitudes, for example.[59] I have made no attempt to place groups of persons in a particular adaptive category and it is assumed that any one person may employ varying "ways out" at times. Nor was it my purpose here to measure and account for the frequency of behaviors. Each of these adaptations was found, though to different extents, in the course of the study. Apathy is at one end of the continuum. Militant unionism is at the other.

Apathy among public welfare staff has been studied and noted elsewhere.[60] In view of the structural obstacles placed in the way of proclient activities and the pressures of work, the effort it takes not to be apathetic rather than the apathy itself is the phenomenon calling for comment. I observed indifference and disinterest at many meetings, and in such behavior as the way workers approached clients in the waiting room. This indifference was also mentioned by supervisors in their descriptions of some workers. Apathy may characterize a worker's total approach to his job or it may be operative only at certain periods.

Secondly, a rather matter-of-fact, businesslike approach to the dimensions of the job attributes rationality to agency procedures and requires only that the worker complete the procedures efficiently. It permits the worker to feel she is meeting her commitment to her client through her own competence. One supervisor said: "I think the best way I can do my job is to be aligned with the administration and abide by the rules." Another stated: "We do our job well and give the clients all that we can."

Closely allied with this posture of efficiency is the conviction that all clients should be treated alike, but this goes even further in protecting the worker from the inroads of the bind. It is important to point out that though rules are supposed to be applied equally, many regulations are established to allow for exceptions (e.g., the whole area of special needs). The equal-treatment credo precludes the person's mulling over the system's basic inadequacies. If rules are to be applied equally across the board, he is not faced with the problem of their being even more inadequate in one situation than in another.

This approach is related to apathy in that it is also more trouble to make exceptions. A worker came to a supervisor for approval of a client's request for a bed. She had made a home visit and presented, almost passionately, the client's dire need of the bed. Citing an administrative ruling, the supervisor denied the request, and the worker was obviously upset that her efforts and the client's expectations had come to naught. Apathy or the "no exception" viewpoint would keep a worker from consideration of such requests and from experiencing the full impact of the bind.[61]

Placing the onus on the client also relieves the bind. As discussed earlier, this position has received both lay and professional support. The professional proviso is that casework services be offered to help the client, yet when service is not effective this is often attributed to the client's characteristics. The staff thus has considerable backing for this view of where the problem lies. One supervisor acknowledged that grants are too low, that workers have no time for services toward rehabilitation because they are too bogged down with eligibility. She feels clients should try harder nevertheless. "Instead of spending so much time and energy in protesting against agency policies, they could use that energy to find work and get off welfare." The lay version is "Why can't those able-bodied women work?"

Distance from clients may not be an adaptive mechanism in the sense of the others considered here, but as a structural circumstance in the agency it does shelter staff from the tension of the bind. Those workers in the AFDC division whose work is not related directly to money grants (e.g., medical care units) said that their situation is different from the other units and that they do not feel (nor did they appear) so harried by client and agency pressures. Furthermore, those supervisors one notch above the supervisor-worker units are removed from clients and do not get the case-by-case pressure. Distance is, of course, an effective screen. One can also contrast the emotional reaction of the worker whose client was not to receive the bed she needed with higher level administrative meetings in which discussions of forms, referrals, procedures, new regulations seem devoid of concern for the people they will affect.

Professionalism in the sense of an individual, clinical approach to clients operates in two ways as an escape from the bind.[62] The professional relationship between client and worker is first of all a mechanism that helps the client to adjust to her situation. Many workers see this relationship as their primary contribution, especially as a means of soothing client-agency disagreements. If that relationship is good, no further outlets, such as welfare rights, are needed.

Further, professional judgment rather than the recipient demand takes precedence in decisions about special needs. As this study ended and separation of services and eligibility was going into effect, it was planned that service workers, not eligibility staff, would make decisions about special needs and so professionalism in the sense discussed here will continue to be important. The worker makes a professional evaluation of the client's need—for furniture, a housekeeper, taxi to the doctor, etc.—and this is done on a casework basis of what is best socially for the family. One supervisor stated that the primary rationale for the social worker in public welfare is to make sound social evaluations.[63] This psychosocial orientation, however, was not universal among trained workers. Many of them talked of clients in professional terms—ego strengths, motivation, psychosocial adjustment and the like—but others stressed their clients' severe poverty.[64]

Some outlets for the bind are primarily venting mechanisms that provide psychological relief. One of these is cynicism—about agency operations or about larger community problems. A supervisor in an administrative meeting said that the only hope for the solution of the agency's personnel problem was a genuine effort by the director to influence the city's governing board, but he had no expectation at all that this would occur. An upper-echelon person told a group of supervisors that clients suitable for rehabilitation were to be referred to a special services program, but since it was known that workers had literally no time to read records carefully and make appropriate judgments, she just would expect that "some cases or other" would be submitted. Many others made both pessimistic and sarcastic remarks about the agency and the welfare system in toto.

A further outlet was the widespread effort to place the blame elsewhere, usually on a higher rung of the system's ladder. This was by way of stating directly or indirectly to clients: "I would grant you what you need if it weren't for these other people." The worker tells the client that the amount of the grant is all that the welfare commission allows. The welfare commissioner says he is restricted by the state's limitations and that the budget has been slashed by the city's financial commission. A member of that commission says the real problem is that the state gives the city no tax relief and his colleagues place the ultimate blame at the door of the Supreme Court, whose recent rulings—especially regarding residence requirements—have swelled welfare caseloads. Of course, each of these assertions may have some basis in fact, but each is also effective in getting people off the hook.

Mutual support in work groups is a well-documented aspect of the informal structure of any organization [65] and serves its psychological purpose here as well. Such was evident in group discussion among workers, in observations made of them at their desk, in informal talks at coffee breaks and lunchtimes.[66] There seemed also to be a special support deriving from the supervisor's antiadministration and politically cynical stance with workers.

Collusion might be considered the ultimate exit from the bind. If agency restrictions do not permit the client's needs to be met, the worker detours around these regulations and gets the needed money to his client. Collusion usually has a clandestine connotation, but the kinds noted here did not have such a character. It was more an open acceptance that there are times the agency looks the other way so that clients can somehow manage. The agency knows, and this was said in a division meeting, that money designated for training expenses in work rehabilitation is often used by families for living purposes. A worker states to the welfare commission that general-assistance clients actually pay much more for rent though regulations require that they secure (unobtainable) less expensive accommodations. (Open collaborative activity between staff unions and welfare rights groups to further the recipient cause might be considered another version of collusion, but this anticipates their entrance on the scene.)

There is a kind of "palace revolt" in which middle-management personnel try to force agency changes and so relieve tensions. A group of supervisors walked out of an administrative meeting, demanding that the agency end a bottleneck preventing the hiring of much needed staff: "We were just like the striking students but it worked." Such effort may be sporadic but gives a sense of direct impact on an overload of pressures.

Finally, there is concerted and continued union militancy, a characteristic of many urban welfare departments. In this one, their felt presence in the agency appeared out of proportion to their actual numbers. An observer is continually aware of their activities: disruptions and challenges both within the agency and in public meetings, flooding of the agency with written material expounding their viewpoint of events almost as they occur, and the assumption throughout of an antiadministration, prorecipient stand. The impact of their activity is twofold: The bind is eased for the members themselves as they engage in actions partly intended to force the welfare system to provide more money for recipients. Further, other staff may make a more political assessment of the agency dilemma as a result, as others might turn with even more conviction to a professional or administration viewpoint.

This, then, is the range of adaptations to the bind observed in the course of this study: apathy, efficiency, equal treatment, the client as the problem, distance, professionalism, venting mechanisms such as cynicism, projection of blame and emotional support, collusion, administrators' rebellion, and militant unionism. No claim is made that this is the full range, or that the only purpose served by these mechanisms is the relief of the bind. These are hypotheses about how staff handles the inherent welfare dilemma. All levels of the welfare structure have been included in this discussion since welfare rights organizations prod each level.

It may not be possible to show a specific association between a particular adaptation and a particular response to welfare rights pressure, but the range of responses will find their counterparts in the range of adaptations. For example, the professionally oriented worker will deny the need for welfare rights organizations as long as the casework relationship has been a constructive one and will look to improved casework services to dilute the impact of welfare rights pressures. The workers active in a militant union will see welfare rights in political terms and help to secure agency directives to aid them in their pressures.

As welfare rights activities enter this account, certain overall effects are evident. By the nature of their demand that staff be accountable to them and not to the welfare institution, they illuminate the anticlient orientation of the welfare system. Because they stress the inarticulation of the social system rather than the shortcomings of individual recipients, they reject the traditional, professional interpretation of the welfare problem. Before the full discussion of the impact of demands based on this stance, agency rules need consideration in their own right, for that is where the action is. Rules constitute the bonds of staff and the target for recipients. The drama of demand and response is enacted in their terms.

CHAPTER THREE

Welfare Rules

Rules are the sinews of the welfare system as well as the arena for interactions with welfare rights organizations. They can be both resistant and vulnerable to the pressure of recipients; this kind of incongruity is their hallmark.

They are a ubiquitous force that holds the system together, and yet their complexity and overabundance strains the system at many points. They are meant to be essentially impersonal and universally applicable, but they are also elastic enough to accommodate different personal situations. They are elaborate and exacting to preclude arbitrary action by staff, but because they permit individual interpretation, arbitrariness abounds. They prescribe precisely what the system can offer its clients, but the overwhelming work needed to meet that prescription makes even that minimum amount difficult to provide. The rules hold the staff accountable to administration and to the public, but there is reluctance to include the system's beneficiaries in that public. All these factors also reflect the contradictions that contribute to the bind, and it may be no accident that they do.

Rules are related to the bind in a further important aspect, one that concerns the potential quality of the bind discussed earlier. Staff can be subject to the strains of the bind when demands from, or feelings about, the recipient situation erupt and cause conflict with agency requirements. That potential makes it necessary for the welfare institution to so create and proliferate rules that staff will be effectively deterred from permitting prorecipient convictions to hold sway. Rules then are as much a function of distrust of the worker as of the client. There may be some concern that staff's arbitrary actions will result in abuses to the recipient, but this is dwarfed by the more compelling concern that liberality will go unchecked. This careful look at the nature of rules is therefore as much to understand their effects on the workers as their use by welfare rights groups.

From the recipient's viewpoint, the rules define the limitations of her life on welfare, and in ways often mysterious to her control her life. They are also what welfare rights groups are attempting to change and so their construction and interpretation become relevant to the kinds of pressures these groups bring to bear and the responses to them by staff. It is a substantial irony that the same set of rules, aimed at controlling clients and workers alike and made public to allow for accountability of staff, are now used, in a more public way than the system would like, by recipient organizations to attempt some control of that system.

First, taken as a whole, the rules reflect the social status of the welfare organization and thereby the bind, as delineated here. All organizations seek a social base,[1] but it is distinctive of this bureaucracy that it is oriented not to its clientele but to the public at large. The institution itself and the rules that govern its operations, then, are responsive to the broad societal attitudes, already discussed, that derogate the beneficiaries of the system. Effects are seen in the kinds of policies and programs established and in the manner in which administration and staff are attuned to the "ground sounds of public reaction." [2] Rules are thus first seen as reflective of this kind of social base.

Further, the directives applicable to dealings with clients control workers as well, and it is this tie of rules to clients and to the bind that is stressed.[3] The overall effect on staff is to stifle proclient activity by the nature of the rules and the effort involved in compliance to them. Though clients of all social agencies are molded by the agency's rules to act like a "case" if they are to receive service,[4] here, of course, this molding is of a much more intrusive, depreciating nature. What makes this undue control (as contrasted with other rule-applying agencies) is the lack of power of the recipients and the fact that the system can be cavalier with them.

Those with the greatest direct contact with the lower class seem most bound by rules [5] and the central theme here suggests why this is so for those affected by the welfare system. The result is conflict for the worker, within himself as well as with his professional colleagues. Several studies have found case-workers overwhelmingly opposed to the eligibility procedures of the agency and feeling caught between those regulations and efforts toward rehabilitation of the client.[6] If the worker wants to "take the role" of the client, he must inevitably challenge the rules,[7] and there is evidence that the final resolution of the tension is often greater bureaucratization.[8]

In any event, there is conflict with a professional stance. For superimposed on the whole configuration of rules, control, and societal attitudes has been the rhetoric and official position of the social work profession that, given trained staff, quality casework services can be offered to welfare recipients. (Part of the impact of welfare rights organizations has been in calling social work on this.)

The reconciliation is attempted through a redefinition of the situation so that the values of agency and profession coincide. A Federal commission recommended against separation of financial eligibility and services, stating that determination of monetary need may very well involve a social service.[9] Researchers suggest that once eligibility determination is complete, "a relationship on a different level can be offered, which the recipient is *free to reject.*" [10] The ruling to notify law enforcement officials of a father's desertion is declared to be in the child's interest and a reinforcement of family ties.[11]

All this seems an effort to include somehow what Hughes terms the "dirty work of the profession" [12] within its more acceptable regions. The results are doubtful indeed, but they emphasize the last of several points offered about the welfare rules in a general sense: (1) that they reflect the special kind of social base maintained for the welfare system; (2) that their nature and extent cause conflict in the worker vis-à-vis his client, whose interests she cannot champion; (3) that the worker is also caught between the demands of her job and of her profession.

Rules are not seen simply as entries in a manual. What their purposes are, where they come from, how they change and how complex they are, how staff interprets and adheres to them are all part of the interchange between staff and rules.

THE PURPOSE OF RULES

A dual conception of the purpose of rules—of manifest and latent functions—follows from much already discussed. On the face of it, rules are rational. Their promulgation is the only way that impersonal, equitable decisions can be made about people in need. Rules protect clients from arbitrariness and abuse. Their manifest function is to make certain that the applicant can be granted the aid she needs in a fair way and as a matter of right.

Welfare rules may be compared to those of other public bureaucracies. The inspector of a motor vehicle department wants proof of the applicant's age, of his knowledge of driving regulations, and of his ability to drive a car. The Internal Revenue

Service requires written verification of the taxpayer's income and deductions and, in an audit, check stubs and receipts as further proof. There is nothing untoward in a social institution's expectation that the citizen will provide appropriate documents and other evidence of his compliance with institutional requirements. We may complain of the extent of these requests, but the propriety of the need for proof is not at issue.

What is different here is that the role of the person meeting the exacting regulations of welfare is a degraded one in contrast to the wholly acceptable role of applying for a driver's license or submitting an income tax return. Rules related to such a degraded status have a correspondingly different purpose.

The latent function of the welfare rules is thus to discourage persons from entering and remaining in that role. The consequences are the means test, and of a recipient's having to "prove" to the worker that she needs a bed or a housekeeper. Some of the responses of the general public to red tape as reported by Gouldner—the violation of privacy, the resentment at not having a claim taken at face value, a sense of powerlessness—are compounded in the welfare situation, since the recipient is in such a vulnerable position.[13] And from the worker's side of the desk, carrying out these simultaneous functions leads to the incongruity of being assured that the regulations are for the client's benefit and that she is entitled to aid if eligible, but knowing that the recipient cannot subsist on the grant offered and that the closed case is the valued one.

The additional latent function is the one mentioned at the outset of this chapter: the control of the worker and particularly of the propensity he might show to act on humane concerns.[14] Rules not only are used to tie the workers' hands, but the situation is so structured that staff members are constantly on call to justify their actions, based on rules, upward through the institutional hierarchy. One can see the tightening of the bind when proclient interpretation of rules puts the worker in conflict as to where his justification for compliance with the rules should be directed—to his supervisors or to his clients.

THE SOURCE OF RULES

The source of rules becomes not merely an organizational matter concerning which level of government sets policies and programs, but of how this separation bears on the nature and stability of rules. The Federal requirements for statewide coverage, for state financial participation, a single state agency (either administrative or supervisory), fair hearings for those denied aid, and certain methods of administration and reporting essentially just set the stage for case-by-case regulation. The caseload is more directly affected by the several-inches-thick state manual outlining procedures on much of eligibility determination and case management—on income, on decisions about real and personal property, on budgeting, on renewals, and so on—with frequently issued directives concerning modifications. Much of the paperwork, but not all, ensues from the statewide regulations. However, it is at the local level that we can see an immediate connection between local conditions, community opinion, and rule changes.

A division chief tells the welfare commission that the department should respond to the demands of the city's finance commission for reduced spending because of a citywide financial crisis, and urges the welfare commissioners to approve considerable restrictions on eligibility for general assistance, thereby of course altering the rules drastically. One commissioner who voted against these cuts later appears before the finance commission and to their insistence that they are not interfering with the internal operations of the department responds that, by their budget cuts, they are in effect making rules for the agency.

As compared with manuals prepared in advance and which will apply fairly stably to recipients, there can be these shifts in the local funding situation with consequent dramatic shifts in rules. As a group of supervisors are in regular meeting, a phone call comes through from a higher administrator. The substance of the call is that, because of decisions just made at the city's finance commission, there are to be immediate changes in the homemaker program. A supervisor tells his group of workers that he has just received notice that because of cutbacks arising from the city's money crisis effective immediately the agency will no longer pay for replacement of clothes stolen from recipients.

Rules are drastically altered and needs no longer met: the stolen clothing is not replaced, the needed housekeeper is not provided, the single, employable person is not aided in general assistance. The workers, of course, are the ones to tell clients face-to-face about each of these changes, and so with an increase in unmet needs there is a corresponding increase in the basis for the bind. Workers talked of the difficulty of explaining to clients that help formerly offered could no longer be given. As far as clients were concerned, their need was the same.

Perhaps as important as the restrictions themselves is the lack of stability in them. One can imagine an easier resolution of the conflict about unmet recipient needs in a situation when rules remain fairly constant and workers can reasonably depend on their continuing stability. The opposite condition is true here, making the accommodation that much more difficult. Workers walk in one day and there is a notice on the bulletin board stating that checks will no longer be held for the client at the agency. This is not a response to a budget cut but rather an attempt to deal with a monumental traffic jam of people. Among other causes, the widespread theft of welfare checks led to an increasing number of requests by recipients who wanted to call at the office for their bimonthly checks, and on those days the waiting room was bedlam. However, the point here is that suddenly workers are faced with yet another directive, which further restricts their ability to meet client requests.

RULE COMPLEXITY

Complex procedures are, of course, not peculiar to public welfare, nor even to public bureaucracies. All large organizations detail their regulations, but there are special circumstances here which tend to increase both the labyrinthine quality of the rules and the pressure to record their every execution. The welfare system's basis in law, the "towering organizational pryamids" created by multilevel governmental auspices, a "dozen supervisory layers" in each department all contribute to the promulgation of rules by the volume.[15] "It is not uncommon," a welfare administrator writes, "to find in some jurisdictions the regulations for one aid program requiring more than one large looseleaf binder to embrace its contents." [16]

Information from this study has confirmed this general view of the extent of rules, and comments by staff members suggest that the burdened reaction to the complexity and volume of regulations is not a function of experience. Many new workers, of course, spoke of being overwhelmed by the sheer numbers of directives and their intricacies, but some veteran employees had much the same reaction. A long-term supervisor, in starting to explain work training rules, said that the details "boggle the imagination" and another admitted that she "just can't learn all the rules." A seasoned supervisor said with some surprise at a division meeting that she was hearing about a (long-enforced) procedure for the first time. In the context of another public welfare study, a welfare supervisor told me that she purposely kept the content of some new directives from her workers because she found it was psychologically impossible for them to absorb the flood of regulations. Some of the subsequent discussion of interaction with welfare rights groups focuses specifically on welfare rights members' having a better grasp of the rules than staff.

Few would dispute the involved and intricate nature of welfare rules or the fact that abiding by them overburdens the worker. There is disagreement however about the function of their complexity. Representative of the view of much of welfare administration is Clegg's statement that the extent of rules reflects "sincere attempts to cover in writing every conceivable human circumstance." [17] Others see complexity as a matter of control and "in the service of our ambivalence toward the poor." [18] There seems little question that the regulations outlining an eligibility determination necessarily require much detailed, personal information about the applicant, given under circumstances of considerable distress in the applicant and a decided power asymmetry between applicant and worker. The effects of red tape on any person—invasions of privacy, powerlessness, mistrust—are compounded for the needy applicants and also affect the worker as inquisitor. Not only the extent of rules but also the intrusiveness which characterizes them, burden the worker and also contribute to the bind.

RULE ADHERENCE

If one were to envision a set of bureaucratic rules, however complex and changeable, and know that they were uniformly adhered to, the question of their equal impact on clients would be relatively unproblematic. A number of factors in the agency studied mitigate against such consistency. At times this is a function of state regulation and outside the agency's control, but often staff pressures and organizational hierarchy lead to deviations in rule adherence.

Internal inconsistencies due to staff pressures, account for many fluctuations in adherence to rules. A state directive with significant impact on client income not only reached the department past its effective date but was also received in units within the agency at different times. There was general acknowledgment in staff discussion that work pressures were such that staff would take this up with recipients at staggered times, so that some recipients will have felt the effect of this rule change weeks, perhaps months, before others.

A supervisor pointed to a pile of case records on her desk, saying this represented a number of recipients with requests for special needs. Because of the recent cutbacks in county expenditures and corresponding restrictions in special needs allowances, she now had to make a strong case for each request, and she wasn't sure when she would have the time to get to all of them.

A legal services lawyer asked the welfare commissioners about a rent increase instituted at the state level (as a result of legal pressure) and made retroactive. Recipients, he claimed, were still waiting for their retroactive payments, due several months before.

These several examples (and many more could be cited) indicate both an uneven application of rules and the effect of agency pressure in keeping clients from receiving what they are entitled to when they are entitled to it. Sparer's comment is to the point: "The right to aid, assuming its existence, is no right at all, if the rent checks go unadjusted, or the wheelchair ungranted for unending periods of time." [19]

Deviations in adherence to rules are also a consequence of one's position in the staff hierarchy, so that in this sense rules have a differential impact on staff. Many workers stated their belief that upper echelons are free to go beyond the rules while they are not. This belief was given some grounding by exceptions made at the top and reversals made by upper level supervisors to the decisions of their subordinates, to be detailed later as responses to welfare rights pressures are discussed.

Reich has charged that welfare administrators "make the law by administrative interpretations under the pressures of current public opinion" [20] and there seems little question that necessarily broad legislation to encompass individual case variations leaves much leeway for administrative rendering. This is one form of interpretation—broadly by the administration for the agency. Another sort found in this agency was a floor-by-floor variety. Many workers complained that treatment of clients varies according to the units workers happen to be assigned to. The implication was that workers, with approval of supervisors, can employ rules either stringently or loosely.

Some supervisors were observed being very exacting with workers, for example, about budget changes or requests for emergency aid, and stated, in addition, that they adhered carefully to the rules. When restrictions on housekeeper aid went into effect, one supervisor placed the blame on the leniency of staff for having granted housekeeper service too readily, thereby contributing to the current financial crisis. Her suggested solution was in the professional tradition—careful social evaluations leading to a more "reasonable" and less lenient interpretation of the rules. Others both behaved and described their behavior as being more lenient, giving both worker and recipient the benefit of the doubt. The nature of the rules allow for this range.

THE UNWORKABLE RULE

Finally, separate consideration is indicated for a set of seemingly unworkable, illogical procedures, which appear to contradict rational bureaucratic behavior or the manifest purpose of services to clients. They are spoken of openly within the agency, and at times at public meetings, giving more legitimacy to claims about them. It is because of their impact on the staff, both in their operation and in their open acknowledgement, that they are included here.

Police verification of stolen checks is described by an agency official as "trying to obtain an unobtainable verification." Monthly statistics are often haphazardly completed and dummy data fed into computers to meet agency requirements superficially.[21] Supervisors talk of instituting a new system for control over assignment of cases, at the same time acknowledging that such control is virtually impossible. Special training courses in casework are arranged for supervisors, not workers, though supervisors neither see clients nor have time to train their workers.

Recipients are to be encouraged toward independence through employment but are allowed only $1.20 monthly for carfare and no allowance for a telephone. A project to allow adolescent mothers to complete high school or vocational training, which would lead toward self-support, is stopped in midstream because of lack of funds. The agency finds an unused directive that could provide housekeeper services for many more families and acknowledges that, with somewhat different procedures, it could receive substantially more in Federal reimbursement for AFDC families with unemployed fathers.

It is not my role to evaluate or comment on reports of these procedures in terms of mismanagement or to imply that such operations are unique to this agency. Though an administrative review of several years ago was critical of this agency's management, a nationwide report encompassing twelve agencies in six metropolitan areas documented widespread inefficiencies.[22] This is an endemic problem. This inefficiency is bound to have an effect on staff orientation to administration and on their potential vulnerability to charges by welfare rights groups about the inequities and incongruities of rules.

WELFARE RIGHTS AND THE RULES

Welfare rights organizations say that rules are there to be used by them as well as by the agency. Their intent is to establish their rights in relation to rules and to influence the power imbalance. They insist that the rules be known to them and that decisions be made on the basis of their demands and not social work judgments; in addition, they seek out unused rules to activate.

This stance is in marked contrast to the majority of recipients to whom rules are mysterious and out of reach.[23] "With most of our clients," a worker said, "we tell them what the rules are and they accept it." Welfare rights groups insist on knowing not only the content of the rules but their source as well and with legal backing, they demand a say in how they are enforced.

In a sense, they have the system in a corner. They cannot be denied access to the rules (although efforts were initially made in this regard) because these are public and, as discussed above, there are important societal and administrative reasons why rules are specific and accessible to certain publics. When recipients insist on the execution of a rule or the revival of an unused one, the system cannot very well deny a commitment to rule adherence. Yet the response of the agency is not merely refusal or acquiescence to demands, but is in fact quite complex. The range of responses depend in part on how the staff takes into account the new kind of challenge that welfare rights groups bring to bear. That appraisal precedes the responses in both the actual interaction and in this report.

CHAPTER FOUR

The Recipient Demands

"In a sense, the government has done one significant thing," Cahn wrote in commenting on the Economic Opportunity Act of 1964.

> much as it did in the Civil Rights Movement, i.e., it has legitimated a grievance. It has legitimated the concerns and grievances and needs of a group of people whose concerns we have never considered to be worthwhile or legitimate before. What has happened, then, is that a process has been unleashed.[1]

This chapter places Cahn's observation in the context of welfare rights activities and elaborates on the "process unleashed" when grievances previously unvoiced demand to be heard. Two major results ensue, distinguished in this analysis but interlaced in actuality. The welfare staff evaluates the demands in a number of ways: are the demands legitimate? are they reasonable? is there power behind them? are they based on the system's rules? In the very process of making these considerations, of giving credence to the grievances, changes occur in the way these two groups—the staff and the recipients—have traditionally interacted. Of these two aspects—the appraisal of demands and the transformation of the relationship—the second may in the long run be the more important, for as usual modes of interaction are altered, evaluations of subsequent demands are inevitably affected. Management takes a far different view of the complaints of the union now recognized (albeit reluctantly) as official representatives of its workers than of those same grievances under their previous relationship.[2] The welfare system's responses to demands are tied to such overall changes in the terms of their interaction.

Since the groups involved in this inquiry are part of a national movement, their position as such, as well as the way they make demands, are background to the staff's appraisal of all they do.

WELFARE RIGHTS AS A NATIONAL MOVEMENT

Welfare rights groups developed nationally in the latter 1960s, a time of mushrooming citizen participation, and were probably in a large sense triggered by the Civil Rights Movement. They received intellectual backing from social work circles [3] and "major impetus from neighborhood-based anti-poverty workers." [4] In 1966 only scattered groups were in existence; by late 1969 the national office could claim 200 groups in 70 cities in some 37 states.[5] Their activities frequently make headlines, their members are called to testify at governmental hearings, and their national executives are consulted on high-level welfare planning.[6] Though some groups have no formal affiliation with the national office, they no doubt still reap the advantages of the increasing awareness of welfare rights as a national movement. It is assumed that a worker's assessment of a welfare rights demand was not unaffected by the appearance of George Wiley, then executive director of the National WRO, as spokesman for recipients on a nationally televised discussion of President Nixon's welfare proposals.

The welfare rights movement is seen by some as a potential force of considerable significance. Though perhaps overstated, predictions relate to the central theme of the bind. There are expectations that clients may "accomplish in their own way, some of the changes that the [social work] field has long advocated" [7] and even that the organized poor would become "therapists for society, uncovering paralyzing internal conflicts and releasing society from them." [8]

Welfare rights demands, however, still represent a prodding, not the wielding of power. To place the groups in this inquiry in some national perspective, one can say that welfare rights are part of a growing national movement about whose future some are quite optimistic but whose membership still constitutes the very small minority of recipients and who are far from the "constituency" stage.

A special circumstance, however, qualifies the limited view of welfare rights' "power" position. Their close collaboration with legal services offices has given welfare rights groups both a sense of power and a role in altering policies and procedures. In fact, many informants said that it would be difficult to separate the effects of welfare rights pressure from those brought in concert with poverty lawyers.[9] Members of welfare rights groups and those of the legal services staff often appear together at public meetings. The welfare staff is fully aware in individual encounters with welfare rights members that legal buttressing for welfare rights demands is only a phone call away. Poverty lawyers give welfare rights considerable status.

THE NATURE OF THE DEMANDS

Welfare rights groups goad the system at many places. They plead individual cases by accompanying their members to the agency to put pressure on the worker, or the worker's supervisor, or the supervisor's supervisor. (New supervisors reported that the groups would sometimes seek them out as being particularly vulnerable to pressure.) Defiantly they go over the worker's head and climb farther up the agency ladder; at times the worker ushers them there. (Some outcomes of this leapfrogging will later be shown to be dysfunctional to the system.) Group members will insist on seeing the division heads, or the director himself.

Occasionally, welfare rights members appear as a group at the agency office to make demands applicable to many recipients, but in contrast to previous periods, this is infrequent and peaceful. For the message came through clearly from all sources that times have changed.

Some workers spoke of the period several years earlier when physical harassment was characteristic of welfare rights pressure. Long-term workers reported such incidents as being threatened with a knife, of being pushed to the ground, of being held prisoner in an office. Frequently, welfare rights groups would picket in front of the building and in the halls; and they would march through the upper floors, normally out of bounds to recipients.[10] This kind of militancy has been described as characteristic of the early periods of many other welfare rights organizations.[11]

The current change in the nature of tactics does not, however, imply a lack of activity, for in addition to individual advocacy, including representing recipients at fair hearings, welfare rights members appear at many public meetings relevant to welfare issues—at the biweekly sessions of the welfare commission, at committees of the city's and state's governing bodies, and at open hearings of the state's welfare department. Clearly, the primary intent of these appearances is to press the recipients' viewpoint on all welfare decisions, but there are subsidiary aims as well—to secure publicity for their efforts and to indicate their sophistication about community processes, not only to use them for welfare rights purposes but to force into the open the antirecipient actions of the governmental bodies and the welfare bureaucracy. For example, after having demanded a say in the welfare commission's agenda for some time, welfare rights groups pressed the issue by serious disruptions that led to an adjournment of one of the commission's sessions. By the next meeting, the groups had arranged for full television and newspaper coverage; all the news media that day carried the story of the commission's adoption of the welfare rights agenda and an item-by-item consideration of their demands. In another series of appearances at both the welfare commission and the city's finance committee, welfare rights groups used the issue of allocation of local funds for school clothing for AFDC children to demonstrate the community's priorities in funding (new uniforms for policemen, a multi-million-dollar expenditure for baseball stadium improvements rather than clothing for children) and to display the recipients' awareness of the efforts of each of these governing bodies to lay the blame for the decision at the other's door.

The thrust of all their tactics is to establish the organized recipients' stance as a rightful contribution to the establishment of welfare policies and of the rules that enforce them. For most of the staff—for those closest to the recipients and therefore most vulnerable to the bind—that pressure comes in the form of individual advocacy. Everyone concerned must take the challenge into account in some way.

APPRAISAL OF DEMANDS: LEGITIMACY

The first obvious assessment involves the legitimacy of the claim, and among the attributes of legitimacy the congruence of the demand to the system's rules (in this rule-dominated institution) would seem primary. The staff would be hard put to deny a claim that clearly fell within regulations. Many workers reported little question about meeting a welfare rights demand if it unambiguously followed the rules, especially if the recipient was conversant with the regulation. A client sought welfare rights advocacy when a question arose about her ownership of a car. When the welfare rights representative made clear that the recipient needed the car for work—a fact the recipient had not stated but which the advocate knew would permit the car —the matter was quickly settled.

The advocate role to a willing, though unsophisticated,

client is also seen as a valid kind of pressure. The clarification of the car requirement was described as a proper, useful form of advocacy. One supervisor, in fact, commenting on the changing emphases of welfare rights activities toward legal changes and class action cases, bemoaned the possibility that welfare rights might thereby relinquish individual advocacy—its "rightful role."

Some staff members go farther than standards of rule congruence and advocacy to the willing client; they fully accept the notion that any group may organize in its own behalf and bring pressure to bear on institutions. These are the younger workers—the "new breed" some have called them—who have matured during an era of protests and have been educated on campuses where this was the order of the day. They sit in disbelief as older workers express their fears of welfare rights members. Their own welfare experience does not predate welfare rights, and this phenomenon coincides with previously accepted ideas about citizen organizations. They are not struck, as some long-term workers have been, with the incongruity of the organized recipient. To them such organization is natural and proper.

In contrast, a number of conditions bring the legitimacy of welfare rights demands into serious question. There is first of all a reluctance to acknowledge the recipient as an acceptable partner in the welfare enterprise. This is most clearly evident in public meetings. It appears not only improper but also unnecessary to legitimate their demands. On several occasions, welfare rights representatives pressed for inclusion in planning or programs—e.g., a committee on the aging, participation in a volunteer program—and these requests were not so much refused as dismissed. This is not to ignore situations in which welfare rights are included—for example, among other instances, they were invited to participate in a community committee on children's services—but rather to indicate that under certain circumstances their demand for such participation can be summarily considered, in some sense, out of order.[12]

Considerable doubt about legitimacy is also raised when the staff believes that the recipient is being exploited for welfare rights' purposes alone. The recipient then is seen as a reluctant pawn of the organization and the demand is deemed improper. One worker recounted an incident with a "volatile, disturbed client" who was pushed "over the brink" by welfare rights' urging of her to make demands of the agency. Others said that welfare rights organizations often raise clients' hopes by giving them the impression that the agency will help even when the organizations know the rules don't permit this. By pressing clients to demand enlarged benefits, the organizations are seen as fostering dependency. The organizations are described as soliciting membership from unwilling clients and otherwise exploiting them.

A tie between professionalism and this matter of exploitation also challenges the legitimacy of the demands. The extent to which the worker maintains that casework handling could have precluded the welfare rights demand is the extent to which the worker questions the genuine need, the validity of the pressure. "Welfare rights membership spoiled our relationship—before then, my client and I could have dealt with this together."

Finally, serious doubts exist about legitimacy when it appears that welfare rights actions extend beyond the individual case, or even the class ruling and legal battle, to an attempt to change the entire system. Extreme disruptions of agency operations, interpreted as an attempt to "destroy the system" as well as indoctrination of recipients to an overall assertive stand against the agency—"they tell the clients that aid is their right and they should make demands"—are seen in this light.

In sum, the rule-aligned demand, the willing client, and the general acceptance of protest support the claim for legitimacy. The incongruity of recipient participation, the reluctant client, the preference for a casework resolution, and the fears about wholesale change erode that claim. More than this, staff decides whether demands are to be considered reasonably presented. For there are particular circumstances here—an institution that gives only negative status to its beneficiaries, a staff encased in a bind about unmet needs—in which there can be marked sensitivity to how the message, however legitimate, comes through.

THE REASONABLENESS OF DEMANDS

To some staff members, any assertion by a client, any behavior outside the role of the passive recipient, is considered a demand in its most aggressive sense. The client has no real right to protest. The staff is doing all it can. Even when the client's right is acknowledged, however, the staff resents the assertion implicit in the demand that the worker is not concerned enough about her client. One can now begin to see how welfare rights pressures strike at and intensify the bind.

Staff members are annoyed that welfare rights attitudes and actions make it seem that "all we are doing for them is not enough." There was considerable agreement, for example, that welfare rights pressures make the job harder for staff: "I know there is not enough in the grant but they should not make demands on us"; "They start yelling before I have a chance to help." One worker said that having constantly to explain to clients the severe limitations of agency policy, was painful enough. These difficulties increased when the workers were confronted by an aggressive welfare rights member: "They make us feel as if the rules are our fault"; "What I most resent is being treated like a stereotype. Welfare rights don't recognize that I am an individual social worker trying to help." Any demand can therefore be interpreted as an assault on the worker's humane stance. One worker wondered whether many welfare rights requests were simply an attempt to get some individual recognition from this impersonal, harried institution.

Over time shifts occur in workers' perceptions of welfare rights demands. Some workers said they had been initially "turned off" by the manner of the demands, but that as they became familiar with the severe restrictions of agency policies they became more sympathetic with the need to protest. Others have had the opposite experience: agency limits made them more hardened, self-protective, and prone to bristle under welfare rights pressure.

Specific requests can be clearly out of line. The unreasonableness is related to the terms of the request rather than the manner of presentation. For example, a client's request for costs of a sitter for a child old enough to be a sitter herself or the demand for a duplicate set of household furnishings when two generations are now to occupy the same home—however presented—can be dismissed on its merits.

By and large, however, the most intense staff reaction—a universal one that crosses lines of hierarchy, or pro- or antiadministration orientations, of agency tenure and the like—was extreme aversion to overtly expressed hostility by welfare rights members. It is of course a natural human response to dislike being subject to yelling and verbal abuse, and in this institution of widely divergent views it was found to be true for the militant unionist as well as the welfare commissioners. There was general opposition to the all-out verbal barrage. At the least it was considered a "waste of time"; at the most, a severe impediment to any resolution of the problem. Until the pitch lessens, the request, however well based, is considered unreasonable.

The congruence of demands with rules has been noted to lead to the perception of those demands as both legitimate and reasonable. The negative evidence of this consisted of complaints that welfare rights members had incorrect information or misrepresented rules. Most annoying of all was the members' "not knowing the rules and yelling anyway."

Staff members can also be annoyed when welfare rights members know the rules too well or too soon. The rules discussion noted both the complexity and the steady stream of welfare directives and the difficulties all staffs have in keeping current.

Staff members are then irritated when recipients are more familiar with regulations than they—"and can quote us chapter
and verse"—and particularly when they cite a directive which
is in effect but hasn't reached the worker's or the supervisor's
desk (or cognition). Staff members know that welfare rights
groups have arranged to receive all new directives as they are
issued and reluctantly admit that they have more time to absorb them. A label of "unreasonable" can be applied when welfare rights members, though staying within the rules, exploit
them to the hilt.

THE POWER QUESTION

Beyond the issues of legitimacy and reasonableness in the staff's
evaluation of the demands is the question of whether a particular demand represents power. Is there strength behind the welfare rights claim to which the institution must show some respect? The point was made earlier that welfare rights groups do
not have the power inherent in a true constituency. Their use
of the system's rules, however, is a form of power leverage. Reminded or informed of rules by recipients, staff members must
bow to these regulations. In that sense, though not mirroring
recipient strength per se, their knowledge of how to use the bureaucratic processes constitutes a measure of power.

Although there were great variations in the perceptions of
the organized strength of welfare rights groups, there was still a
general acknowledgement that the groups were bona fide organizations and not just a handful of disgruntled clients. Some
staff members attributed changes in policies and procedures to
their efforts.

Many comments indicated an impact out of proportion to
their numbers, and a perception of a more extensive, better organized network of groups than other observations would support. This may reflect what has been termed the organized
poor's "disconcerting effect on public attention.[13] In addition,
the buttressing afforded the groups through their collaboration

with legal services would also add to this sense of strength. It was in these two respects—the ability to disrupt and to muster legal support—that the element of power entered into staff's considerations of demands. These two possibilities were potential resources for the groups and the staff was aware that they were always in the background.

EFFECTS OF THE DEMANDING PROCESS

In the process of weighing demands, the balance of relationships is upset. When a person who has never made demands before begins to do so, she not only changes, but she also affects those to whom she has traditionally been subservient.[14] Merely taking those demands seriously enough to weigh their validity and appropriateness gives stature to the demands and to their authors, and throws a different cast on usual client-agency relationships. Whatever happens after that will be affected by the way the parties have been changed by the demanding itself.

What occurred in this agency in this regard may best be described as the substitution of a demand structure for the traditional command structure. By the latter is meant the usual kind of interaction between staff and welfare recipient wherein staff explains and enforces rules with little expectation of challenge or question from the recipient. The demand structure upsets that manner of relating and replaces it with an encounter in which the previously servile recipient, bolstered by an organization, no longer accepts the premises of the passive role and in fact replaces her submissive behavior with a pressuring stance. The following discussion presents evidence that this is so, suggests how this change comes about, and comments on what consequences ensue. This shift does not imply that recipients now command, but only that now their demands are taken into account. This, of course, is the point made just above— that the act of considering demands, in and of itself, and even before the agency responds, alters relationships.

Indications of modification of the "command structure"

came from several sources, the common theme being that now the staff had to consider the possibility that the organized recipient might challenge actions at any time and want a say in decisions. For example, a supervisor said that before the advent of welfare rights, she had only to be concerned with meeting the expectations of those in the hierarchy above her. Now if welfare rights are involved in a case, she must worry about them as well. Another supervisor acknowledged that workers included welfare rights demands in their judgments about exceptions to be made to rules. A number of persons stated that the possibility that welfare rights organizations might question procedures or bring pressure to bear means that workers have to be "on their toes" much more and have to know the rules more thoroughly. There was, in a sense, a felt presence of the welfare rights groups and a posture of being prepared for challenge. Even a practical matter such as waiting room procedure shows similar effects. When a client appears accompanied by a legal services attorney or with a person known to be from a welfare rights group, the worker is summoned immediately. This is in contrast to many other situations, in which a worker's coffee break or dictation time is honored and the unaccompanied client may wait.

This modification of usual interactions appears to evolve in two ways. First, by knowng the rules, welfare rights groups can intrude upon the traditional relationship. One can judge the utility of such familiarity with the rules by visualizing the complaining but unsophisticated recipient. She is not effective because the worker can simply tell her that the rules do not permit acquiescence to her demand. Even if she pressures those farther up in the hierarchy, she will be met with the same rules, given additional confirmation along the way. The anger around the demand can also more easily be dealt with as an indication of the client's psychological problem rather than on the basis of the request itself. Backed by awareness of regulations and legal services if needed, the welfare rights member, however, cannot be sloughed off as the usual hostile client can. Many of the staff members, for example, said that the angry recipient of yesterday is often the welfare rights member of today, but that the two situations cannot be dealt with in the same manner.

Secondly, these are not individual complainants but members of organizations. Granted the distinct lack of welfare rights political power vis-à-vis the welfare system, the agency is still sensitive to what power they can muster in terms of public presentations and legal support. This potential for organized disruption makes the usual individual resolution insufficient.

The knowledgeable, organized recipient cuts through the traditional authority relationship. The worker can no longer make decisions on his interpretations of the rules alone or on the basis of a casework judgment as to what is best for the client. The staff must modify its professional role and does so very reluctantly. "Arousing their self-respect as citizens," Gellhorn writes of the organized poor, "has meant seeking to change the donor-donee spirit, a change not always palatable to the donors." [15] It had been a jolt to this agency staff to have "another person sitting there in the office with the recipient, citing regulations." [16]

The earlier description of agency rules would certainly indicate that although the individual worker is not without controls, those controls ordinarily remain closely guarded within the system's network of rules. Welfare rights intrudes from the outside.[17] Demanding intensifies the bind, and most staff members reacted to whatever pressures recipients bring. Workers said they didn't like to be reminded of how restrictive the policies were; demands backed by knowledge of the rules make that kind of attack more severe. At welfare commission meetings, welfare rights leaders could speak knowledgeably about the way in which recent cutbacks would affect the young unmarried mothers now unable to finish training, of how changes in the disability program would affect services to those recipients, of how state regulations were to be altered. At a welfare commission meeting, a welfare rights leader read aloud to the commissioners a statement issued by the agency a few years previously, taking a very strong position on the importance of adequate services to clients. She charged that these service needs were unmet and that the agency was not doing the job to which it had pledged itself. In sum, the organized recipient, aware of the system's workings, can, by her demands, contribute to the bind.

It may seem that staff members viewed the activities of welfare rights groups only from their own vantage point, particularly in the sense of impact on them and on their conflicts. This was not so in many instances, and some of the comments hinted at what might be termed the "transformation of the demanders" (a subject for study in itself). Recipients are helped and changed, staff members said, by having recourse to the organizations ("at least now they have a choice as to where to take their grievance") by being able to gain a sense of power through group action—or at least the companionship available there—by having the organization serve at times as a stepping-stone to employment. Ascribing this at least partly to welfare rights activities, a supervisor said that "AFDC clients just look much better these days." Many of the staff seemed aware that the effects of making organized demands are felt not only in agency offices but elsewhere in the city.

This chapter—the evaluation of demands and the transformation of traditional interactions—is not only preparatory to an account of agency responses, but it also considers them separately in the conviction that describing the responses without looking carefully at the implications of the demands themselves would miss much of the process. This would seem especially true, since the making of demands by organized recipients is a recent phenomenon that would seem to require attention in its own right.

CHAPTER FIVE

The Agency Responses

The impetus for this study emerged from my interest in whether welfare rights organizations have any effect on the welfare system. It would appear that the answer may be found in the specific responses the system makes to welfare rights demands and that therefore a straightforward inquiry into what the groups ask for and what the system grants would be sufficient. But it is evident from the discussion to this point that such an approach would be an oversimplified distortion. Many of the features of the circumstances in which demands are presented and addressed are problematic. To understand and explain what effects ensue from welfare rights pressures, it is necessary to take into account some of the major systemic conditions impinging on the staff and the variable aspects of accommodations to them. The bind, the staff's adaptation to it, and the special qualities of welfare system rules have been considered as two of these major conditions and have been seen to have varying consequences. Further, the demands have not been taken as given, but also are differentially affected by staff's evaluation of them and by the implications of the demanding process itself. The system's rejoinders are related to these factors and are similarly problematic.

The answer to another version of the initial guiding question—do welfare rights groups have any significant impact on the welfare system?—seemed similarly not to be found in the mere accounting for the success or failure of particular assaults on the agency. To see this phenomenon more dynamically, responses and their consequences can be described in terms of impact on continuing agency operations. The agency's responses could then be categorized into two groups: *functional* and *dysfunctional*. The former are those which absorb, dilute, or smooth out the pressures so that routines are left undisturbed or, if changes do occur, agency operations are enhanced. The latter are those which lead to disruptions of such a nature that the staff is made uncomfortable and the system operates with more difficulty.

Beyond being an appropriate and heuristically useful way of describing sets of responses, the categorization is pursued for a larger purpose. In the long run, it would seem important to students of the phenomenon of the protesting disadvantaged clientele and the ponderous social institution to know something about whether the first group can leave its imprint on the second. For the heavy bureaucracy, that imprint may best be judged by the ability of the clientele to have its viewpoint significantly alter the normal institutional machinery. The impact of outside social forces on organizations has been well discussed in the literature, as, for example, the consideration of cooptation below will indicate. However, it seems important to emphasize both here and later that the social force trying to intrude in this situation is a stigmatized population, not, as in other instances studied, a group of some consequence.

Social institutions resist change and encroachment by others, even (and in this case especially) by their beneficiaries. The basic requirement of an organization is the maintenance of its integrity and the continuity of the system itself. First among the strategies for meeting that requirement is the protection of the organization's security against external social forces.[1] In some circumstances, such threats might involve an onslaught against the organization by forces strong enough to have far-reaching effects: to change its policies or organizational makeup or sources of power. In this situation, it seems more reasonable to stress those aspects of organizational resistance which are more in keeping with the recipients' potential for disruption. Here this would be on the lower, but still significant, level of procedures.

Because bureaucracies strive to achieve predictability and to maintain internal controls unscathed by outside forces, any meddling in the institutional routine is perceived as a threat.[2] Resistance to such interference has been seen in a variety of service institutions (particularly relevant here) in which "dysfunctions for the public do not evoke the concern of officials preoccupied with operations."[3] Mention was made earlier of the fear of the unpredictable and uncontrollable intrusion of parents in the school system.[4] A study of nurses identified the "home guard" as a group with some power within the institution who resisted the "episodic interventions" of outsiders, in order to minimize discontinuities of work.[5] The high-ranking civil servant will rebuff even socially desirable reforms because they "disrupt the continuity of practices and interpersonal relations within the department."[6]

The special circumstances of the welfare system make this commonly observed institutional resistance even more steely. Much of the previous discussion of the bind, particularly as to the derogation of the recipient, can help to explain the unique disdain for interference from these "outsiders." When confronted with the recalcitrant individual client, the bureaucracy avoids him because he "gets in the way,"[7] and when faced with recipient groups, "containment and direction are, in fact, the strategies which bureaucracies typically employ in response to low income groups which impinge on them."[8] The condition of the stigmatized population thus encourages the effective resistance of both the individually unmanageable recipient and her organized neighbors. Not only do organizational require-ments then take precedence with little heed to the recipients' needs but the concerns of the two can be so disparate as to in-tensify the institutional opposition to client incursions.

> The problem of staff turnover, hard-to-reach or overly demand-ing clients, vague service objectives, dull and endless staff meet-ings, intra-organizational conflicts, and the general overwork experienced eight hours a day simply are not the same as un-employment, inadequate housing, punitive and hard-to-reach services, dirty streets, abusive officials, slick merchants, sick chil-dren, and a relentless, pervasive hopelessness experienced every waking moment.[9]

The premium placed on neutrality by traditional social work philosophy leads to the avoidance of the tensions necessary to bridge this gap. The middle-class social worker can be char-acterized as softening conflict and preferring "cooperation no matter how spurious to conflict, no matter how necessary." [10] Such developments as the emergence of the advocate role in social work, the union activities noted in this study, the social work organizer in community action programs challenge this characterization, but these are still only a small part of the social work enterprise.

In addition to the disparity in concerns, the derogated client intimidated by the middle-class institution, and the conflict-eschewing staff, the agency administrator who must make a "highly politicized effort to maintain his own survival and that of the agency" adds another imperative to institutional resis-tance to client interference.[11] For, of course, the kind of politi-cal pressures with which the administrator must deal do not de-rive from the recipient groups.[12]

Thus an impressive roster of conditions mitigates against recipient impact. Indeed, the agency finds a number of ways to turn those pressures into agency-oriented outcomes. Some re-sults of these interactions, however, prove dysfunctional to the system, and further, even some aspects of the functional responses strengthen the welfare rights groups, if only indirectly. For one of the many hypotheses of this report is the conjecture that any legitimation of the recipient groups increases their viability and potential force. Some of the institutional responses —particularly the uses to which the agency puts the welfare rights groups for its own purposes—cannot help but add to that legitimation. Blau suggests that bureaucratic officials are compelled to make adjustments to external dysfunctions only when the resolution of these outside conflicts are transformed into organizational needs.[13] A modification of that comment is offered here—the outside groups can come to serve the needs of the agency, thereby effecting to some extent an unanticipated resolution of these external problems. Supporting evidence for this view will be presented in discussions of the dilution of the demand and the utility of the groups in terms of those responses to welfare rights activities which are functional to the agency.[14]

A comment is in order about an overall ad hoc impression concerning agency behaviors. Though this inquiry did not extend to any agency planning session regarding welfare rights organizations, the evidence available pointed to the absence of a deliberate strategy in dealing with the groups. Rather, particular tactics seemed to evolve in response to specific situations.

FUNCTIONAL RESPONSES:
THE ABSORPTION OF THE DEMAND

The first set of responses works out well for the agency because, in these, pressures can be so absorbed or blunted that no appreciable accommodation need be made in how the agency usually goes about its business. To begin with, the institution can, and does, essentially disregard the demand. This occurred on a number of occasions at welfare commission meetings when welfare rights requests on different issues were summarily dismissed. It also was evident when demands to workers or supervisors for exceptions on individual cases were easily refused, as being clearly outside regulations and requiring little attention. Representing somewhat more of an agency involvement, but still minimum, is the management of the demand via casework strategies. The pressure is taken more seriously, but not as a concerted intrusion on procedures. It becomes a situation requiring individual attention. Instances were cited of the "reasoned discussions" with welfare rights complaints, with an amicable, unruffled resolution as far as the agency was concerned. In the same vein was the suggestion that an important agency role was "building the ego strengths" of welfare rights leaders so that they can learn how to deal "reasonably" with community agencies. Some of the staff referred, cynically, to the public relations function of the community division as "caseworking" the sharpness out of the welfare rights demands.

An interesting contradiction of views arose regarding the rationale for the community division. Those most directly involved in the division stated that its primary purpose related to community relations generally and not the "management" of welfare rights groups, and that, in fact, its establishment predated the emergence of these groups. Others were convinced that "community" was a euphemism, and that the division was specifically activated because of the need to "cool out" welfare rights organizations. The contradiction seemed somewhat resolved by a third viewpoint, which held that even though welfare rights groups postdated the community department in time there were welfare rights rumblings in other communities nearby and the division was established in anticipation of its occurrence in this city. This kind of management smacks of a "cooling out" process that did, in fact, characterize a number of other agency actions.

Cooling out, as used here, is meant to convey the notion of a device by which individuals are effectively persuaded to accept failure of their efforts or at least to accept less than they had in mind.[15] It might not seem like failure when the agency makes individual concessions in order to forestall trouble. Such handling, however, does effectively take the wind out of the sails of organized action, while leaving the demander with a sense that her demands have been satisfactorily met. This is a well-worn bureaucratic tool—"concessions to individual clients to avoid the challenge of the administrative ruling which affects many people." [16] Commenting from a legal viewpoint, Grosser and Sparer note that the "gratuitous granting of case-by-case accommodations actually provides the public agency with a viable strategy for maintaining the status quo, for it disarms the practitioners without establishing precedents and thus vitiates issues." [17]

Many instances were cited of exceptions made in individual cases, as well as the placement of welfare-rights clients' requests ahead of others'. "I don't bypass any regulation but I work on the request faster if a welfare rights person is involved"; "I put through the request faster to stop the screaming and get them off my back"; "There seems to be an unwritten law to handle these requests quickly, primarily to forestall further trouble." Several references were made to what was termed the "hot line" to the director: an arrangement whereby some welfare rights leaders could reach that office directly to resolve complaints. A supervisor reported a welfare rights leader had complained that although this direct line did get results for the individual case, "somehow" all the others with the same need were left unaffected. When the leader continues to accept the individual resolution without pursuing the class case, the cooling out strategy has been successful.

A further mechanism is to deflect welfare-rights demands. The tendency of many persons within the system to place on others the blame for the institution's shortcomings, as cited earlier, is one aspect of this. However, the groups are at times specifically advised to direct their fire elsewhere. In a public meeting, a city official tells welfare rights groups, who are urging increased welfare expenditures, to "mount a campaign and take it to the state." The welfare commissioners exhort the groups to send to the state legislature petitions pressing for the adoption of a bill that would increase state participation in local welfare costs. The agency representative at an appeal procedure urges the welfare rights member there to carry on the fight to the welfare commissioners for greater county allowances on individual budgets. Several workers report telling those of their clients who are active in welfare rights to try to change restrictive laws, and a supervisor says she is convinced, and tells clients so, that welfare rights groups will be much more effective in the long run if they address their protests to officials at the city and state level instead of "hammering away" at the agency. A worker says that whenever possible he tries to reroute recipients' anger from him to the punitive policies themselves, and he encourages them to attempt to change these policies.

Note that these tactics may ultimately be dysfunctional for the system, for there is the potential of changing operations or at least of encouraging a stronger welfare rights movement, if not in actuality then at least in the sense of power felt by welfare rights members. However, for most of those who employ this tactic, especially those mostly concerned with routine procedures, this is not an outcome to be reasonably expected. The most obvious result of their strategy is that their operations will be left untouched. Of course, for many, the exhortations may be mere rhetoric.

The mechanism of co-optation characterizes other agency tactics, but for it to fit here the concept requires some modification from its classic exposition. The case used as grounding for Selznick's discussion involved a force of considerable social strength outside the institutional structure so that co-optation in that instance could be accurately defined as the reflection of "a state of tension between formal authority and social power" [18] and as a process of absorption of outside elements in order "to avert threats to [the organization's] stability or existence." [19] Because those elements did represent power, the price the organization paid for that accommodation was to "be shaped in turn, to submit to pressure upon policy and action." [20] Since the outside groups in the welfare instance are not a constituency or a power bloc, one would not expect a real threat to the institution or recipients' molding of agency policy as a consequence of co-optation. The mechanism operating here also falls between formal and informal co-optation as defined by Selznick. There did not seem to be a need for the establishment, in open terms, of the "administrative accessibility of the relevant public" [21] or for the informal elimination of opposition.[22] Still, the concept can be usefully applied here because it clearly denotes the strategy of absorption—here not so much to deal with social power as to impair the capacity of the outside group to prod the institution.[23]

Indications of co-optation were to be found in the actual inclusion of welfare rights members in the workings of the welfare system, as well as the encouragement of a kind of collegial association. Welfare rights groups were represented on a number of committees within the agency itself—for example, to plan guidelines for special needs allowances, to work out procedures for the implementation of an educational fund ruling, to plan children's services. They served on many citywide committees as well—e.g., housing and urban problems, community action. Staff members who had worked in welfare departments elsewhere reported an even greater incorporation of welfare rights groups there, to the extent of their being used as orientation personnel for new staff, as well as being housed in offices within the department's building for easy accessibility to recipients.

The collegial quality occurred in individual associations—a supervisor, for example, reported that after a stormy beginning, her relationship with a welfare rights member developed into that of two professional colleagues working on a problem of mutual concern. Evidence of this cooperation could also be seen in the community division, where the official policy was to work cooperatively with welfare rights organizations, among other community groups. Staff representatives frequently attended welfare rights meetings, where they acted as liaisons to the department. Some staff members contended that the agency, as a co-optation device, had arranged for a job in a related welfare agency for a prominent welfare rights leader. Other members hotly disputed this assertion. However the job had materialized, the leader had nonetheless become part of the city's welfare structure.

An offshoot of each of these agency actions is that, in the process of co-optation, the groups, by being brought into the welfare system, are legitimated. Besides committee work and liaison arrangements, the staff makes referrals of individual clients to welfare rights groups much as they would to other community agencies, lists of welfare rights organizations are posted in the department's offices for easy reference, and workers note membership of clients in welfare rights groups in a matter-of-fact way in case records (including, as in one example, its therapeutic value to an isolated AFDC mother). In a letter to the local newspaper, a commissioner approved the role of welfare rights groups in bringing client complaints to public attention. Indicative of the limits to this legitimation, however, is that there are no written procedures governing welfare rights agency interactions. Perhaps this encourages flexibility, but it also precludes challenge on what has already been legitimated.

Even without such formal symbols of legitimation, this by-product of co-optation is not insignificant. The major point of difference between co-optation in the usual sense and co-optation here will make this clear. The outside group is not only without social power, it is also without a sanctioned social role. Far from a matter of absorbing powerful elements that threaten the agency, here the question is whether recipients have any valid social status at all. Any social mechanism, then, which makes use of the group's activities confers a measure of social value on them.[24] Now, as other functional aspects of the agency side of interactions with welfare rights groups are described, consequences for the recipients—particularly effects on their status—begin to be evident. In a strict sense those agency actions to be considered are not responses to demands per se, although they may relate to elements of the demanding process —e.g., the use the staff makes of welfare rights members' knowledgeability of rules. They do represent agency behaviors still essentially functional in outcome—i.e., nondisruptive to departmental procedures or involving those changes with no consequent discomfort to staff. However, aside from dulling the edge of prodding, these actions have other uses for the staff. The outcomes provide economies for the workload and enhance the worker's role, and by doing so, they similarly increase the social worth of the welfare rights' activities. For in many ways, use of welfare rights groups makes life easier for the staff.

FUNCTIONAL RESPONSES: THE UTILITY OF WELFARE RIGHTS

Welfare rights groups are a source of information not only to their own members, but also at times to staff. New workers have learned about agency procedures from welfare rights members. For example, when both supervisor and senior supervisor were ill and unavailable, one new staff member often used welfare rights groups as an information bank: "If they didn't know the specific rule, they could tell me where I could find it." Her supervisor confirmed that this was sometimes a valued contribution of welfare rights in view of the welter of procedures a new worker had to learn.

They frequently help to resolve problems around eligibility and budgeting. A welfare rights representative convinced an angry client to accept the need to obtain an estimate before she could be granted a special-need allowance for a household appliance. A recipient suspected of concealing information from the agency was persuaded by a welfare rights member to provide the true information—which, in fact, established her eligibility. Another recipient, shifted between divisions because of confusion as to which category of aid she was to receive, sought the aid of a welfare rights advocate who "came in and cleared this up in no time." The episode of the car requirement cited in the earlier discussion of demands is another example of clarification of eligibility. Many instances were mentioned of welfare rights members' usefully interpreting rules to recipients. Welfare rights representatives seemed more aligned with agency than recipient when they calmed an emotionally disturbed client whose bizarre behavior was making a determination of eligibility impossible. A staff member went beyond the limits of agency operations by referring a neighborhood problem involving some unscrupulous merchants to a welfare rights group, because "this was something that needed organized action."

Welfare rights groups also explain to recipients their rights and entitlements. In view of all the work demands on them it seemed to staff both reasonable and useful for welfare rights groups to provide this service.

This is the only place they can find out about special needs— except in special circumstances, like a baby's birth when I ask about crib and layette, I don't have the time to find out if they need anything extra.

We just don't have the time to explain all they are eligible for.

There may be other, agency-oriented reasons for the lack of explanation. "After all, we just can't lay it all on the table and say 'take what you like.'" However, even for this last worker, as well as other time-pressured staff members, it was considered proper for welfare rights groups to provide information and encourage recipients to claim all their entitlements. "I refer clients," one worker said, "just so that they can know their rights." There is value, others said, in welfare rights meetings where "recipients can compare notes and know what they may be eligible for." Welfare rights groups, a commissioner said in open meeting, have been "very helpful over the years in letting clients know what they are entitled to."

It seems appropriate to digress here for a moment and comment on a contradiction that has probably become obvious. The chapter on demands made very clear that, by and large, staff members disliked being pressured by welfare rights demands. Yet here there is evidence that staff members approve of welfare rights groups' informing group members of all their rights and entitlements and encouraging them to claim these rights. Clients are even referred for just that purpose. Interestingly, this apparent contradiction frequently existed in the same person. This paradox is perhaps best exemplified by the worker who said that she often refers clients so that they know their rights but "I only hope they don't come back and yell at me." Further, it seemed clear that workers did not view this combination of attitudes as a contradiction. They spoke of their anger at demands, and the reasonableness of the rights and entitlement functions of welfare rights in the same, outwardly unconflicted, breath. It might be argued that knowledge of entitlements does not in and of itself lead to demands that can't be met, that such claims might be readily allowable in the normal course of events. However, many of them do relate to special needs, and special needs—particularly in tight times—can remain unmet needs. In addition, an overall encouragement of the notion that the recipient has rights contains the potential for ever-increasing demands on the agency. Perhaps the contradiction evident here is not viewed as such by the staff because the welfare rights stance reflects that component of the bind which is their humane concern for recipients, which their reactions to demands must at times not overshadow.

Finally, among the uses of welfare rights groups functional to the staff's workload is one of a psychosocial nature. Referrals are made when clients seem very isolated and need the psychological support of fellow recipients. Both the informal and formal discussions are also seen as helpful in recipients' adjustment to life on welfare—e.g., in managing on the budget or in dealing with schools and other community institutions. More than just a gathering of neighbors who happen to be recipients, the groups provide support and information and potential organized strength. Pressures on the staff to attend to psychosocial problems are thereby lessened, and workers see accruing to clients benefits that they know the agency is not in a position to provide. In this, and the matters of information and eligibility and entitlements, welfare rights are sources of workload economy. Other interactions with them may also serve to lighten the worker's burden in less practical, but perhaps more meaningful ways; her role may even be enhanced.

A familiarity with the rules bolsters welfare rights demands, but it also gets the worker off the hook very effectively. Now rules, not workers, receive the blame for the agency restrictions, and the worker's position is thus legitimated. "They can see we're not lying and that it's not our fault."

"I used to make trouble for my worker," a welfare rights member announced at a state department hearing, "until I realized that it was the rule, not my worker, that was the problem." So the worker is off the hook and to the extent blame is placed elsewhere, she is somewhat out of the bind.

Other responses may also relieve conflict as well as avoid disruptions. Workers sometimes relieve the intensity of pressures of demands by the mechanism noted earlier: they simply suggest that recipients take their complaint one (or more) steps up the agency ladder. Whatever the outcome there (and one version falls in the dysfunctional category) the worker is temporarily out of the middleman position and his workday continues without further disruption. In other instances, the worker may not refer the recipient elsewhere in the agency but so manage the recipient's hostility that he has the same sense of escaping from conflict. "I just stood firm with this angry client—I learned a lot about how to withstand this kind of onslaught"; "This kind of recipient used to unnerve me—now I can just let her rant and it doesn't bother me." Especially within the context of a proadministration orientation, this kind of response to demands increases the worker's feelings of confidence in his ability to fend off disruptions.

Apart from any response the staff may make, welfare rights activities in and of themselves favorably affect worker roles by relieving staff members of some of the intensity of the bind. There was some acknowledgement that pressures welfare rights bring to bear are welcome because grants are so low and policies so restrictive, and that staff and recipients are really after the same thing. In this sense, the groups are perceived as fighting the staff's battle for them. And in the several ways mentioned above whereby the outcomes of the interactions are economies in the workload, the staff is thereby relieved to some extent of one of the work pressure components of the bind.

LEGITIMACY AS A BY-PRODUCT

A thread runs through this explication of functional responses, touched on in considering the legitimation by-product of co-optation and of the uses of welfare rights groups, but requiring a more careful look. It may be that one of the more important issues in considering welfare rights impact is the legitimation of recipient organizations. A step upward for any disadvantaged protest group is taken when those with greater social power acknowledge that the organization exists and has some legitimacy. Beforehand, a sure way to dismiss the protest is to deny the rights of groups even to present their protests. One can imagine that if the first of the functional responses noted—a disregarding of the demand—were effective, the need for the rest would not arise. Ample evidence exists to support the long-standing social view that recipients have few rights as recipients and certainly no right to protest.[25] Whatever alters that view and enhances the acceptability of the movement increases its effectiveness.

Welfare rights groups gain legitimacy in several ways. These are presented now in descending order of deliberateness on the part of the agency. The first is a more or less carefully weighed decision to sanction the organizations. An administrator mentioned that, in the early days of physical harassment, her suggestion to meet with the groups to ease the situation met with resistance within the agency, on the grounds that so to meet would have acknowledged the organization as a bona-fide group. When the decision was made to arrange such a meeting, there was then a conscious, though apparently mixed, judgment to admit the group's existence and to deal with its members in some way. The legitimation that evolves from co-optation is a less deliberate matter, because the purpose of the strategy is the absorption of the demand, but legitimacy does come in its wake. Finally, there is a sanctioning of the groups —a kind of "creeping legitimation"—which evolves not from demands (the sanctioning is in fact only related to demands indirectly) but results from other purposes the groups serve for the agency. The economies for the staff workload and the enhancement of the worker's role are in this category.

Further, it is clear that these several versions of legitimation occur simultaneously. It may well be that simultaneous with the welfare commissioners' refusal of a demand for committee representation or city officials' denial of the request to seat a recipient on the commission itself, several workers at the department office are using welfare rights groups in a variety of ways. One is referring a lonely client for companionship, another finds her client at home in group discussion about budget management with other welfare rights members, a third worker, new to the agency and with no supervisory assistance available, phones a welfare rights leader whom she knows is conversant with rules for information needed for another recipient. At one level legitimation may be deliberately restrictive, and at another social value and approval are placed on the group's purposes and activities. The response of the system is not monolithic and legitimacy may accrue in complicated ways.

DYSFUNCTIONAL RESPONSES

The institutional responses so far considered are termed functional because either they do not permit welfare rights groups to intrude significantly on normal operations or they result in alterations of usual routines that enhance those operations. (The legitimation that does occur may constitute a potential threat to procedure but it is not so as yet.) The outcome of other responses was the opposite. In these, the results of the demanding process were disruptive, and included hierarchical disputes, disorders in caseload management, worker-recipient alignments, and actual changes in procedures. The institution finds means to counteract this last effect, but it seems probable that the others may continue to ensue from welfare rights prodding, a matter of considerable interest to the overall appraisal of recipient actions.

Of all the dysfunctional results, emotion ran highest around the consequence of welfare rights members' demanding what might be termed "capitulation of the senior supervisor." The steps common to each of the episodes reported were of the type that follows: a welfare rights representative insists first to the worker and then to her supervisor that a recipient's unmet need be met, by either bypassing or stretching a rule. Both worker and supervisor deny the request on the basis that it is far enough outside regulations to be disallowed. The welfare rights person, with recipient in tow, demands to see the senior supervisor, who grants the request, and the worker and supervisor are left to pick up the pieces.

An illustration will fill in this basic outline with the elements that create the psychological furor. In one instance a recipient demanded a special need allowance in order to purchase household appliances; the worker had refused the request, despite much haranguing by both recipient and a welfare rights member, as contrary to rules. The recipient and the welfare rights member then insisted on speaking directly with the supervisor, who then had to spend a good part of a workday "arguing with them and taking a lot of abuse," but continued to support the worker's decision. The recipients then took the issue to a supervisor one notch higher, who decided to grant the allowance. The worker who had insisted adamantly that it could not be issued then had to arrange for the check.

As staff members recounted such experiences, there were commonalities in the reasons they offered for this outcome and in their descriptions of subsequent effects on workers and supervisors. Staff members claim that reversals occur because supervisory personnel are not exposed to client situations day after day as workers are and have therefore not adjusted to being faced directly with the effects of low grants; and when they are they can't take the hostility of the welfare rights person complaining fiercely about unmet needs. This is the aforementioned "distance" adaptation to the bind, in which higher-level staff members are isolated from the impact of client circumstances, an adaptation threatened here by the welfare rights confrontation. The explanation of the senior supervisor's behavior was given somewhat matter-of-factly, but the effects on worker and supervisor came through at a higher pitch. From the supervisor: "I have to live by the rules and help my workers live by the rules, day after day, and then this happens." From the worker: "I insisted so many times to my client that nothing could be done about this—now I'm the one who has to face her." Thus the reversal undermines the staff's adaptation to rule restrictions and interferes with the continuing relationship with the client.

This experience also exemplifies both the differential impact of rules on staff and the elasticity in rule interpretation discussed earlier. The upper level supervisor was free to interpret the rules in a more liberal fashion than worker or supervisor, without their concern for criticism from supervisors. It is entirely possible, in addition, that the interpretation could have been well justified, in view of the leeway the system permits in application of rules.

Another version of this sequence occurred. Some workers mentioned their own practice of purposely encouraging clients to proceed higher up the agency ladder if they are dissatisfied, knowing—and in fact hoping—that higher echelons may reverse their own decisions. Of course, they are not bothered as others are by the reversals, but the responses of the others involved constitute the disruption. The immediate supervisor may disagree with the worker's intent and the senior supervisor may be both interrupted and troubled by the welfare rights demands. It is important to add that many of the staff—workers and supervisors—stated that such reversals did not occur in their experience. When the reversals do occur, either by leap-frogging or ushering, there is proof to welfare rights groups that decisions can be overthrown, though they may not be so aware as the staff of the repercussions of doing so.

Another kind of disruption for the agency is a direct consequence of the shift of "command to demand" considered earlier. When staff members attend to welfare rights requests quickly (bypassing other clients in the process) so as to "forestall trouble," "to get them off my back," welfare rights groups are in a sense determining the order in which the caseload is served. Staff members said there always have been hostile clients who request attention "out of turn"—the squeaky wheel getting the grease was frequently mentioned—but that here there were other, more compelling reasons to allow clients to pace staff's work—e.g., organizational consequences such as publicity. A measure of control over caseload management thus passes to the organized recipient, and not only usual procedures but also staff-determined procedures are disrupted.

An alignment between workers and recipients has the potential for the most severe impact on business as usual, for it would substitute proclient activities for administration-oriented operations. Even routine referrals to welfare rights groups for clients to know and assert their rights place those assertions above possible subsequent effects on the agency, though these were not the purposeful, active coalitions with more immediate consequences. The two unions active at the agency engaged in a more deliberate partnership, the smaller, more militant organization being the more involved. These union activities resembled what Riessman has termed and recommended as a "third force," i.e., an alliance of professional and nonprofessional representatives of the poor . . . urged as a "third force" mediating between the more militantly organized poor and the institutional agency structure.[26]

Both unions assisted welfare rights groups in practical ways —such as aiding them in setting up their central office—and in a number of issue-oriented activities—such as advocating recipient causes at commission meetings, seeking to fill a commission vacancy with a welfare-rights–sponsored recipient, testifying at public hearings for proclient measures. The unions' frequent exposing and questioning of agency operations at commission meetings served the welfare rights cause, if only inadvertently, by making those operations known to them as well as the rest of the audience. Further, the more militant union was even more actively involved in fostering cooperation with welfare rights groups; their members appeared at welfare rights mass meetings to give information to recipients about agency workings not readily available to them, to plan with leaders for staff members to act as liaisons within the agency, and, as some members stated, to try to show the recipient groups, by example, the effectiveness of the union's method of disrupting agency operations. There was a mixed appraisal among the staff about the motivation of this union; some were of the conviction that the union was exploiting recipients for its own purpose vis-à-vis the agency. Whatever merit there might be in this allegation, the end result was a coalition between welfare

rights groups and unionized staff with observable and potentially disruptive qualities. These kinds of alignments may even
magnify the sense of disruption, since they represent a conscious acknowledgement that the staff is more accountable to
the recipients than to the administration.

Finally, specific changes in procedures evolved from welfare
rights pressures. There was no clear consensus among the staff
about attributing these procedural changes to welfare rights activities exclusively (their collaboration with legal services was
frequently cited) but the contribution of the groups was generally not denied. In the period before cutbacks in local alloca-
tions, the groups were seen as instrumental in broadening the
special needs area to include many more goods and services for
clients. The more efficient issuance of emergency checks was attributed to their pressure, as was the change in rules about se-
curing estimates for the purchase of some household furnishings. Reactivation of an educational fund ruling was a most
prominent result of their activities. Beyond these kinds of specifics, their presence may have effected overall, more diffuse
changes which have come about, as one worker said, "just because we have to be more careful about abiding by the rules
and because they force things out in the open." The welfare
commission sessions are no doubt of a different character than
they were in pre-welfare-rights days, and in that sense, too,
usual procedures are altered.

Each of these dysfunctional changes may have differing effects on the bind felt by the staff. It may be that reversals at a
higher level and the by-products of expediting the demands
will intensify the bind for some workers by interfering with
their usual adaptations—by disrupting the way they "live by
the rules" in the one instance and with their control over their
own caseload in the other. The other dysfunctions may have
quite the opposite effect for some staff. Those union workers
actively in alignment with welfare rights groups are relieved of

the pressure of the bind by this proclient activity and even more of the staff may be similarly affected when liberalized procedures are put into effect.

THE SYSTEM'S COUNTERMEASURES

The welfare system of course does not stand mute and immobile when its operations, particularly its control over such operations, are threatened. The countermeasures noted in the course of this inquiry would appropriately be considered functional as defined in this analysis, for they manage disruptions to the agency's disadvantage. I shall discuss them separately now to emphasize that they are counterreactions to welfare rights effectiveness.

First, the system can simply rescind any specific regulations activated by welfare rights pressure or can so revise procedures as to make a prorecipient success unlikely. For example, in collaboration with welfare rights, legal services effectively pressed for a change in agency procedures whereby a supplementary check granted on an emergency basis for food in one month was not to be deducted from the recipient's check in the following month. The agency's response was to eliminate emergency orders almost entirely.[27]

The agency also tries to deter staff–welfare-rights interaction. When two workers were suspended for having met with a welfare rights delegation, for example, a supervisor warned her workers to restrict their encounters with welfare rights members to individual conversations.

Finally, as an example at the state level, the considerable increase in the number of fair hearings has been followed by a correspondingly increased number of "alternate decisions"—a euphemism for a higher-level reversal of the hearing officer's findings, which usually results in a denial of the recipient's claim. The purpose served by these alternate decisions is apparent in view of the observation that "the state hearing officers are more client-oriented than anyone at the local level," [28] and that a sequence of such client-oriented decisions has been known to influence policy.[29]

A CASE IN POINT

A resume of one particular issue may serve to integrate a number of factors that have necessarily been considered separately throughout these chapters. This might be termed "A Brief History of the Life and Untimely Death of an Inactive Rule" and concerns an educational fund ruling. By following the sequence of events surrounding its enforcement and subsequent removal from the books, the rule's history can illustrate the related elements of the demanding process.

The rule, inactive for many years and in fact never really implemented, permitted an AFDC family to set aside for present or future educational purposes income other than the AFDC grant, such as child support or social security payments. Activation of the rule can be seen first as related to the bind. Rather than just administering niggardly grants from month to month, workers could collaborate with clients about both present and future educational needs for their children, which might reasonably offer some hope to AFDC families. The rule had both logic in its ultimate purpose and an element of respect for recipients not too often apparent in welfare operations.

The issue is a clear illustration of welfare rights knowledge of the rules and, in coalition with legal services, of the capacity to make appropriate demands based on rules, for it was their demand which actuated the rule. It is, of course, not unrelated to the basic character of the welfare system that such a rule, especially with the potential for cutting through the generational cycle of dependency, had remained dormant. The demand, then, was based on a rule and as such would have to be considered legitimate by the staff. Presented in a legal framework, it also bypassed problems of reasonableness which might be associated with the hostile, individual complainant.

The system institutionalized the demand and was able to

partially control the outcome by setting up machinery, though with welfare rights participation, to effect its implementation. Hearings were held at the state level—here unions were aligned with recipients in support of the regulation—and committees were established within the agency (again they included welfare rights representation) to establish guidelines for the rule's use. Though there were some complaints from staff members about the prolonged nature of this phase—"It took months and months to put this rule into effect and 24 hours to rescind it"—the regulation was finally applied to a considerable number of families.

The order to rescind was announced dramatically at a welfare commission meeting as a letter from the state department was read aloud, and the coalition of welfare rights, legal services, and unions was vociferous in its objections. The implementing directive went into effect soon after, though with unevenly timed effects on recipients.

One might say that was that and file away the sequence as an interesting example of the process under study and as an illustration of the welfare system's capacity for countermeasure. However, I believe that the processual elements in this example will continue to be operative in further welfare-system—welfare-rights encounters and that the outcomes of the demanding process cannot be recounted and measured only in terms of a particular pressure and a particular result. The uses to which welfare rights groups are put and the transformation of both sets of participants as the demands are made are illustrative of this more complex view. Responses are integrally related to the other phases of the process, and in that sense, whatever the particular response, those elements—the bind, the rules, the demands, and indeed, other responses—will continue as potential forces to effect future interactions.

CHAPTER SIX

Catalysts for Change: Issues of Professionalism, Vulnerability, and Dehumanization

One of my aims in this book has been to describe the demanding process; a further aim is to extend it both conceptually and practically to address the concern for humanization. The process of interaction helps to achieve the larger goal of humanization in two ways. The first is that client pressures force a penetrating examination of the welfare institution—not as official rhetoric would have it but as it is from the recipient's view. Organized recipients see through professional jargon and charge that the staff have been carrying out the latent, but to the client the real, purpose of the institution. These recipients will not permit the staff to continue to do so. Secondly, welfare rights groups, by their very actions, illustrate the proposition that humanizing efforts can be initiated from below. Further, the analysis of the consequences of their demands suggests strategies that staff members themselves might use. These two outcomes of the demanding process—the insistence on honesty about the staff's role and the offer of both a model and specifics for change—will be the links to be exploited here to join this one instance of client pressures to the wider question of humanization.

Client demands do not constitute the only way in which questions are raised about purposes and practices of such organizations as the welfare system. For example, such challenges arose in War on Poverty programs, which the Federal Government itself had originated. The activities of the staff unions in the agency studied illustrate another source of such challenges. These alternate wellsprings do not, of course, detract from the particular effects of recipient-initiated demands.

Client challenges, which compel an undistorted view of this social institution, can lead to humanization, because if one is going to humanize this or any other social instituion, one must first view it uncompromisingly. Demands for humanization imply that staff members have not been treating clients with respect for their integrity or with their interests foremost.

To what extent this is so and why this is so are questions to be addressed first in this chapter, which takes seriously the claim of organized recipients that the system has not been accountable to them, and which pursues the implications of that claim. I believe that one explanation lies in a faulty professionalism in public welfare. Partly because the institution has not been answerable to its clientele, as it purports to be—that is, because the staff has not acted professionally—the system exhibits a marked vulnerability to attack. It is the gaping discrepancy between official pronouncements and actual "service" to clients that, after all, puts the staff in a bind. Finally, many factors combine—societal attitudes, as well as inadequate professionalism and an absence of accountability—to result in practices that dehumanize both clients and staff.

The rationale for these discussions is that an examination of issues of professionalism in public welfare, of the system's vulnerability, and of its dehumanizing aspects can serve a catalytic purpose. If those who work in public welfare are to begin to consider humanizing efforts, they need to see the institution as it is, and also their role in making it so, and the dehumanizing effect it has on them. Ways of changing can evolve only from a combination of a sense of dissatisfaction with a sense of direction, both of which may come from this hard look.

PROFESSIONALISM IN PUBLIC WELFARE

To this point, several allusions have been made to the issue of professionalism in the welfare system—the earlier hypothesis about professionalism as an adaptation to the bind, the discussion of the profession's role in blaming the individual recipient rather than society for his status, and the profession's claim of therapeutic results. Now, these strands can be brought together, and with the confluence of other ideas and the questions forced into the open by welfare rights prodding, some reformulation of the issue can be attempted. In addition to the heuristic purpose these comments may serve, they are also meant to be the intellectual context in which later strategies usable by public welfare personnel will be discussed.[1]

Perhaps a useful starting point is Freidson's contention that "the only truly important and uniform criterion for distinguishing professions from other occupations is the fact of autonomy—a position of legitimate control over work."[2] In part, that autonomy is granted, to add Greenwood's views, because society recognizes that the professional's skills are based on a "fund of knowledge that has been organized into an internally consistent system called a body of theory"[3] and this in turn leads to a recognition of professional authority—an acknowledgement that the professional has a particular skill others in society do not have. But the theoretically based skill is not sufficient. The professional's autonomy is legitimated not only when he has "persuaded the state that the occupation's work is reliable and valuable,"[4] but also when society is assured that his skill will be used within a service orientation.

He must not permit self-aggrandizement or other personal or organizational pressures to interfere with his primary commitment to the interests of his client or to the professional imperative that he "must, under all circumstances, give maximum caliber service." [5]

There are, of course, other attributes of a profession, but the ones mentioned would seem to be necessary, if not sufficient, conditions for transformation of an occupation into a profession.[6] This property of autonomy based on theoretical knowledge and a service orientation has been selected for emphasis because it is the point of abrasion between the welfare system and social work's claims to be professional. Ideally a social worker, analogous to the physician or lawyer, on the basis of legitimated autonomy, would be free to provide service to her client, informed by soundly based theory about both diagnosis of and intervention in the client's problem. The client's interest would be the major determinant concerning such interventions.

In view of these imperatives of autonomy legitimated by theoretical knowledge and a service orientation, I believe that in public welfare the profession of social work has not been allowed, or perhaps more precisely, has not allowed itself to act professionally. First, public attitudes toward the poor have dictated the overall diagnosis. The recipient's dependency status has been declared to have been derived from some personal malfunctioning, and although the social worker was free to use his knowledge and skill to determine what particular kind of personal malfunctioning was operative in any particular instance, the aim was individual rehabilitation, not a critical focus on social causation. "In a rehabilitative regime, recipients are moved toward conformity (work and self-support) through the use of benign, professionally sanctioned services." [7] Public welfare programs have been instituted in the light of societal attitudes toward the assisted poor which have given recipients a degraded status and the feeling of personal responsibility for their plight. The essential diagnoses have not been made by the social work professional, and policies and procedures emanating from the basic societal stance assigning degraded status to the recipient and social control to the worker have made it exceedingly difficult for the social worker to place her client's interest first. On these counts, the social worker's ability to act professionally, i.e. autonomously, with full utility of theory-based knowledge and professional authority, and with a service orientation, has been severely restricted.

Dumpson's criticism speaks to this point:

> I wonder, in retrospect, as we focused primarily on intrapsychic functioning of the poor, as we highlighted the internal causation of economic dependency rather than calling attention to and developing strategies to deal with flaws in the economic system, whether we really were not more interested in wrapping public welfare in a cloak of professional respectability than we were in human restoration. We stood by and watched the attempts to implement the 1962 amendments with their interpretation that the causes of dependency were within the individual and his need to be rehabilitated, while many words were spoken about the impact of squalid housing, the poor health services that those on public assistance could obtain, the discrimination they met in every area of living and the immobilizing self-images that the maldistribution of opportunity produced.[8]

There are two necessary clarifications to the gist of this argument about professionalism. First, the service orientation aspect of professionalism is not meant to be defined solely by the degree of accountability to the client. Such equivalence would suggest that the professional accepts the client's interpretation of his own reality as the sole basis for professional judgment. The inference is not intended. There is a body of theoretical knowledge from which the professional draws, and the client's view must be weighed against that knowledge. The argument that the welfare professional has paid too little heed to the client's perspective is not to suggest the abrogation of the right (and responsibility) of professional judgment, apart from that viewpoint. Blau and Scott warn professionals against the danger of permitting clients to dictate conditions of service, though interestingly they add that "failure to serve the welfare of clients is probably a more prevalent problem in service organizations than becoming subservient to them." [9]

Further, the criticism of the social work profession within the public welfare system is intended to be a generally directed one—the target is not the individual worker, who somehow did not challenge the profession. The profession, as a whole, "focused primarily on the intra-psychic functioning of the poor," as Dumpson claims.[10] In doing so, it believed it was acting professionally. It would have been unrealistic to expect many workers to question a well-established professional stance.

To digress a moment, there is a peculiar irony to be noted in this situation. Public policy has been so intent on assigning individual responsibility to recipient status in order to forestall an acknowledgment of other causation, that through the years there has been no demand for proof that rehabilitation programs based on this individual approach do in fact make a significant impact. Congress continually granted money for training stipends and service programs without such proof.[11] Wiltse's early and limited study indicating an outcome of lessened welfare dependency is one of the oases in a desert of inconclusive evidence about the effect of professional casework service in a public assistance setting.[12] Evidence points to a lack of any basic therapeutic meeting ground between recipient and worker [13] and, even in a fairly ideal situation professionally, a significant lack of success.[14]

The attempt to clarify the issue of professionalism in public welfare has centered on two of the basic requirements of a profession—legitimated autonomy and a service orientation. This has been done to raise some questions about the basis of previous claims for professionalism in these settings, and to anticipate questions that may arise in later considerations of a changed stance by the professional toward the recipient, specifically whether that changed stance is consistent with a professional orientation. That consistency will be measured against these selected attributes of a profession.

The present discussion excludes certain areas. The question of professionalism in public welfare has arisen in other contexts than the present one and it seems important to separate those contexts from considerations here.

First, the present perspective on professionalism is not meant to encompass the dilemma between being a professional and being a social activist in the larger community. Some years ago both Bisno and Greenwood warned that social welfare's traditional social-action purpose might be an uneasy companion in social work's striving toward full acceptance as a profession,[15] and recently there have been a number of studies questioning whether social action is possible for and evident among social workers and whether it is consistent with a professional philosophy.[16] It is obvious, certainly, that exhortations for social action among social workers, such as those made by Thursz and Wiener, are consistent with both the viewpoint expressed here about social causation of recipiency status and, as will be evident, with the later discussion of change strategies.[17] However, my intent is to address the problem of humanization of the social institution of public welfare (among others). For this reason, the focus will remain on the institution itself rather than on social action beyond its confines, and particularly on a concern for a different perspective in which professional responsibility in service to individual clients may be expressed.

In addition, the present analysis is not meant to question the appropriateness and validity of any number of services that social workers render individual recipients. Instances abound when, even within organizational constraints, meaningful and therapeutic encounters occur between worker and client. The questions raised here are not intended to depreciate these, but rather to suggest that in the large majority of encounters diagnostic and interventive skills are misused in the service of society's need for social control. The client's mental health (as well as the worker's) may be better served by the use of other conceptions of professionalism and of the use of other than the medical model for service.

Finally, I have not addressed the issue of professionalism through the framework of role orientations. A number of writers have studied such role orientations,[18] seeking to distinguish between bureaucrats and professionals in service agencies. The contribution of those studies to an understanding of a professional stance in social work rests on the assumption that the professional as contrasted with the bureaucrat provides a client-oriented and professionally valid service to the recipient. Through a careful look at the bind and the worker's adaptations to it, I question that assumption.

The professionally oriented worker is described in those studies as the one who bypasses or overlooks rules in order to provide autonomous, client-oriented services. He is contrasted with his bureaucratic counterpart, who aligns himself with the agency and against clients by assiduously following rules no matter what the impact on his client. The adaptation considerations in this study suggest that the professional worker is similarly aligned with the administration, though perhaps in a more subtle way. Though he may decry punitive rules, he plays into the previously described stance of the welfare system—that the problem lies within the client and not in the niggardly grant or the punitive procedures or larger social causations. He also becomes party to a casework practice based on the belief that professional service can be offered by the same person who is also the agent of a nontrusting, controlling institution and without full regard for the effects of that institution on the client's life.[19] In the context, then, of a system which chooses to place the responsibility for the client's situation at her door, which provides for the barest minimum of life's necessities, and which does not acknowledge the contradiction in the charge to control and rehabilitate, the professionally oriented worker who provides and champions services under those conditions can be considered as administration-oriented as the bureaucratic staff. Also, his allegiance to service can be his way out of the bind.

Beyond this limitation to using the bureaucratic-professional distinction to characterize an appropriate professional stance, I have also expanded ideas concerning the bureaucratic position as well. Bureaucratic behaviors were found to be somewhat more complex than previously delineated. The rule follower could be the apathetic worker for whom a violation of the rules would involve extra effort she wasn't prepared to make or the person who rationalized that the efficient way was the best way to make certain clients receive all their entitlements or the worker who justified strict adherence to the rules by the conviction that all clients should be treated equally. Of course, in this rule-applying institution with its impressive ascending order of accountability, workers may stick closely to the rules simply to preclude being called on the carpet. Beyond these variations in bureaucratic perspectives, I believe that the bureaucratic path is also an effective way out of the bind and that this comprises an even more compelling reason for straight-and-narrow behavior than is the case in other bureaucratic institutions. Each of these rule adherents, in addition to being proper employees and acting in what would seem to be a self-protective and rational manner given the circumstances, effectively shields herself from the realization that abiding by the regulations can be harmful to her client.

Having said that this analysis of professionalism does not encompass social action but rather focuses on worker behavior within the welfare system itself, having accepted the validity of some individual attention as now given, and having questioned the usual conception of a professional orientation as essentially proclient, I would like to pursue the selected professional standards set forth above and consider some notions about how social workers might approximate those ideals. The knowledgeable, autonomous, client-focused professional is seen as the goal.

The professional is first of all expected to be well grounded in the theory which is the foundation for his skills. However incomplete social work theory may be, there is no doubt that knowledge of social science has always been an integral part of it. Among other things, this would include knowledge about the social and economic causative factors related to public assistance problems, including the relative place of personal and social causations.[20] That knowledge would also include an awareness of theoretical propositions about the latent purposes of social institutions, specifically how the latent purpose of this institution can be seen as obscuring causal issues. Welfare rights activities force a greater clarity on both counts.

By their public statements and by their personal postures, members of welfare rights organizations make amply clear that they see the existence of the publicly supported poor as a social problem, not a series of individual ones. They challenge the social workers' traditional way of rationalizing public assistance programs by defining them in terms of the individual recipient's difficulty and glossing over the system's need to degrade its beneficiaries. They do not permit staff members to be unaware of the bases of their usual patterns of adaptation.

This staff adaptation is what Merton refers to as one of the alternatives for the intellectual in a bureaucracy: "to accommodate his own special values and special knowledge to the values of the policy makers." [21] This is the process Brager described in writing specifically of public welfare:

> If responsiveness to powerful groups in the political marketplace is a primary determinant of organizational decision-making, then we may expect professionals to rationalize their behavior to these requirements.[22]

This is the spur for Pauley's assertion that

we have not protested with conviction the continuing attempts
. . . to set up public welfare programs that have an underlying
philosophy of contempt for [their] beneficiaries.[23]

These statements speak to societal imperatives which shape the
welfare system and organizational forces which pressure individual staff members to adjust to that shape. Theoretical
knowledge about these interactions should be part of the professional's base of information.

Blau and Scott admonish the professional in a service organization about the potential danger involved in permitting
clients to determine the nature of the professional service.
That can be paraphrased. It is perhaps more dangerous to permit society to determine that service, and more dangerous yet
to be unaware of the process by which it does so.

Being professional in public welfare requires a cognizance of
the societal and institutional factors which inform service to
clients—of economic and social theories concerning public dependency, of organizational theory, concerning not only matters of integral administration but particularly those related to
latent goals of social institutions and the staff's accommodations
to them. It is the kind of knowledge base that tends to be
blurred as social work professionals adapt to what they find in
the welfare system. It should be as much a part of the intellectual accouterment of the social work professional as knowledge
of psychological theories. It is the sort of knowledge recommended in the present definition of the social work professional. Welfare rights groups insist that the social worker see
the system as it is; a body of knowledge can help him to understand conceptually why it is so.

For the other professional necessity considered here, welfare
rights pressures again demand a more professional stance. Welfare rights groups call for the worker's accountability to them
and not the organization—another way of specifying a service
orientation. As welfare rights groups make staff members more
aware of the bind, they are in effect asserting that the staff is

not meeting its professional commitment to place their clients' interests uppermost. In the light of societal and institutional constraints which act to preclude such a stance, this is no easy task for the individual worker. To get a handle on the difficulties involved, it might be useful to examine just a few of the changes necessary for a true service orientation to have a chance of survival in public welfare.

Placing the recipient's interest in a predominant position requires, first, a different definition of her. Much of the present policies and procedures can be rationalized on the basis of both a degraded status for the recipient and, despite pious statements to the contrary, of her posture as a submissive supplicant vis-à-vis the system. It is more difficult to fulfill society's purpose of social control of the recipient, however, if one conceives of her as a rights-bearing citizen struggling with an institution that derogates her. Then, other possibilities evolve. One is then able to see that "to attempt to facilitate a client's adjustment to such a social system is to betray his interests." [24] One is then open to an approach that suggests seeing "every problem the client 'has' as a possible problem the social institution 'has.' " [25] In other words, meeting the professional commitment to the client means that one must be prepared to "protect the individual against the system," [26] and arriving at that point requires first a view of the client in a different light.

A more precisely defined service orientation also raises some questions about professional values. On the one hand, social work professes a commitment to the client's right to self-determination and to a concern for his interests (even in the face of institutions which violate his rights and depreciate his humanity). It is recognized, for example that

> some of these conditions [welfare rules] may be considered as attacks on his integrity, dignity and privacy and the social worker may feel that the results of the authority he has to impose are not consistent with professional principles and values.[27]

On the other hand, social work students are educated to eschew conflict and to view the acceptance of authority as a sign of maturity, so that they are offered neither professional sanction nor the necessary skills to try to bring institutional requirements more in line with professional values.[28] As Rein suggests: Social work values are "problematic rather than self-evident, and frequently conflict." [29]

In sum, then, these discussions of professionalism in public welfare have contended that political imperatives have set the stage for the service of the professional—i.e., diagnosed the problem as essentially individual rather than social and veered the direction of the social worker's commitment away from his clients. To pursue a more professional course, at least two necessary shifts are suggested—a greater conversance with societal and organizational influences that impinge on professional service and—perhaps more difficult to achieve—a service orientation based on an altered definition of the client and a more honest appraisal of values that inform social work behavior. This does not by any means exhaust the conditions for greater professionalism, but rather raises some questions about how one provides service that more effectively approximates a professional ideal within the context of such an institution as public welfare.

An instructive parallel to the public welfare instance is Nonet's insightful historical analysis of the administration of workman's compensation in California.[30] The earlier policies of the Industrial Accident Commission, Nonet contends, had a "social welfare perspective"—i.e., to prevent both poverty and social unrest.[31] There was little legal framework for the claims of the injured worker and, particularly relevant here, his demands for compensation were not taken at face value but were assumed to reflect a "real underlying problem," which the agency was to define.[32] The role of the injured worker was purely a passive one, and it is here that Nonet introduces the concept of moral captivity noted earlier—the acceptance of the terms and consequences of others' definitions of one as appropriately divested of certain statuses and rights. The injured worker was to be given what the agency felt he needed (the assessment of special needs for welfare recipients comes, of course, to mind), and the administration of aid was carefully supervised by the commissioners, who assumed that the man and his family needed direction every step of the way.

Significant to this focus on welfare rights impact is the fact that over the years, as the injured workers were supported by an increasingly strengthened union movement, there was imposed on the Industrial Accident Commission a different definition of the worker—now a citizen with rights to make claims against the company held responsible for his injury and with no assumption made of the right of the administrative agency to interfere in his private affairs. In contrast to moral captivity, the unions by "implanting an adversary procedure" created a "lever to restore moral independence." [33]

Nonet's example is illustrative of several relevant issues: that the clinical model used by an agency which both administers aid and provides individual rehabilitative services attenuates clients' rights; that a different definition of the client, no longer assumed to be responsible for his own plight, alters the administrative agency's behavior; that these changes can result from the impact of outside forces. When applied to public welfare, Nonet's analysis suggests that the implications of "moral independence" permit a clearer perspective on causative elements for recipients' circumstances and preclude the misuse of a clinical model in their solutions. Such an evolution as Nonet describes—the transformed definition of the client, his rights and his position vis-à-vis the administrative agency—permits enhanced professional behavior on the part of staff.

To those with direct experience in the public welfare system, this emphasis on professionalism in that system, particularly as a way to humanize such organizations, may have seemed somewhat off-center and distorted. To say the least, the social work profession's role in public welfare has had an ambiguous past, and so any statements about professionalism there must be placed in the framework of the uneven tie between public welfare and the social work profession. Secondly, there are realistic limits to the responsibility social work can assume for the changes essential to humanizing the welfare system. The next few pages deal with these two issues—the ambiguities of professionalism and the limitations to change—as necessary qualifications to the matter of a different professionalism in the welfare system. Hopefully this will not dilute the main argument, but will place it within realistic parameters.

Public welfare has clearly always been part of the social work profession but has never gained full acceptance. Over the years, very few public welfare workers have had professional training, and until recently only those staff members with graduate training were admitted to the professional organization. Even the professionally trained public welfare workers fall short on matters of status and salary when compared with their counterparts employed in other settings—family service agencies, child guidance and psychiatric clinics, and the like. Yet, there has been little doubt that the social work profession claimed public welfare as its own. Professional conferences and professional journals reflect this claim, many administrative positions in public welfare are filled by fully trained staff, and perhaps most important, the stance taken with the public has always been that professional social work was responsible for the services provided in public welfare departments, even if qualified staff members were chronically hard to come by. As examples of many public statements over the years, social work testimony to Congressional committees at the time of the consideration of the 1962 Social Security Amendments amply demonstrated that rehabilitation services provided by trained social work staff were an integral part of the public welfare picture. The large sums of money granted by Congress through the years for graduate training stipends were public acknowledgment of that professional claim. Even with the anomalous situation in which the vast majority of public-welfare staff was not accepted by the profession itself, many aspired to gain acceptance. Others in and out of the profession believed more trained staff members were the answer to many public welfare problems. Public welfare was clearly the social work profession's responsibility.

The picture has shifted somewhat now, though the tie is still there. Separation of services and eligibility is becoming an established fact of public welfare life and the eligibility workers —technicians as they are sometimes called—may have lower academic qualifications than previous workers, certainly are not expected to have graduate training, and yet will have much of the in-person contacts with recipients.

Still, there are important indications that the social work profession is not relinquishing its territory. Social workers with graduate training hold administrative posts at all levels, and trained personnel will continue to offer casework services. The membership requirements of the National Association of Social Workers include those professionally untrained, but college educated, personnel who are employed as social workers. These requirements are met by many public welfare staff members.

If this agency's plan for evaluation of special needs by service workers is any bellwether, those services will have their financial components, blurring the distinction between services and eligibility. In the foreseeable future, barring the unlikely possibility of some form of guaranteed annual income with public social services administrated completely separately from money payments, one may expect that social work services will be provided alongside financial assistance.

The argument about an altered professionalism was made with the recognition of the recent changes in public welfare administration—separation of services and eligibility—and the long-standing and continuingly ambiguous nature of public welfare's place in the social work profession. These discussions were addressed to, and hopefully will be useful to, both trained and untrained workers, but with special awareness that the social work profession bears leadership responsibility. The conceptual insights spurred by the implications of the welfare rights demanding process, and notions about altered practices similarly sparked there, may have the potential for humanizing this and other institutions, and staff of whatever professional standing may find utility in them.

However, any ideas about internal institutional change must be qualified by a very clear acknowledgment about the part staff changes can reasonably be expected to make in the total public welfare picture. Without that clarity, it could be assumed that this book's stance implies a power social workers and public welfare departments do not possess. They are not responsible for the problems of the publicly assisted poor. The causes of these problems lie elsewhere: primarily in a defective economy; in a mobility-blocked social system affecting all the poor; and, affecting the nonwhite poor, evident racism in employment patterns, in labor union membership, in ghettoed housing and ghettoed education. Nothing of the discussion is meant to imply that social workers in public welfare can take on these burdens themselves. Any internal change within the public welfare system is just one of many possible ways to resolve the problems of those receiving public assistance. Other avenues are admittedly of far greater consequence.

What may be ironic in the face of the above disclaimer of responsibility (readily acceptable to many professionals) is that the social work profession has claimed that therapeutically induced changes in individual clients would make an appreciable difference. "A dispassionate analysis of social policy," Rein comments, "would confirm the conclusion that social work programs have been used as a substitute for more searching policies to redistribute income, power and resources," with these programs based on "the professional doctrine emphasizing therapeutic solutions." [34] and as Turner observes (stressing a "moral commitment" to so state) "this has been an expensive response because caseloads get larger and results remain largely irrelevant to the problems." [35] The argument made in an earlier chapter concerned the misuse of a personally oriented explanation for larger social causation, where the mechanisms of Beck's "welfare as a moral category" and Ryan's "blaming the victim" were seen to be translated into a rationale for professional services. Social work has claimed more than it could deliver, and in the process it has distorted the problem. If public welfare as an institution cannot reasonably be expected to impact the larger problem of poverty, so also must significant change via individual therapy be questioned. As many writers have urged and, more important here, as welfare rights organizations have insisted, the public welfare system needs to take a different stance toward recipients and their problems. Staff may not have responsibility for the formation of these problems, but they are responsible for the consequences of their behaviors toward them, whatever the limited place of those consequences in the total picture.

THE WELFARE SYSTEM'S VULNERABILITY

The issues now to be addressed—the welfare system's vulnerability and, below, the question of dehumanization—encompass in the first instance the properties of the system which make a changed professional stance imperative, and in the second an analysis of what happens to recipients and staff if the change does not occur. The need for another form of professionalism seems intricately interwoven with these two issues.

The interaction of welfare rights groups and welfare staff served to expose the vulnerability of the welfare system in a multifaceted way. The politically oriented workers,[36] particularly their coalition with organized recipients, the effects of publicity forced by recipient demands, the mechanisms involved in the dysfunctional responses, and the exploitation of rules have a common thread—the susceptibility of the system to such attack.

The politically oriented worker—both the one who merely takes a political (and cynical) view of agency operations and the active unionist—rejects both the rules of the institution and the basis on which professional service is offered within the system. He aligns himself with the practical needs and civil rights of clients and maintains a societal perspective on the recipient's problems. This stance, as were others, is also an adaptation to the bind, but it is more of a challenge to the agency. That challenge is to the legitimacy of the agency's values and policies. As Mechanic comments, lower participants in organizations

> will be more likely to circumvent higher authority . . . when the mandates of those in power, if not the authority itself, are regarded as illegitimate.[37]

The potential for this kind of challenge explains for Gouldner the need for the hierarchical supervisory system in social work. That system is required, he believes, because higher echelons must convince the lower ones of the rightness of the agency's basic philosophy.[38] In addition, in her coalition with recipients —by beliefs or action—outside the limits of usual agency procedure, the politically oriented worker forces into the open the conflictual nature of the welfare system.

The effect of this political orientation, which is in fact the effect of welfare rights activities, is based on the agency's susceptibility to attack. In a sense, the agency is set up for such assaults. The potential in the staff to act on its humane concerns and the conflict of this potential with agency requirements were cited as major components of the bind. This tension makes the worker more vulnerable to welfare rights pressure. The tension between the agency's official claims to be a humanitarian enterprise and to provide a climate for recipient oriented professional services conflicts with its controlling and depriving qualities and leaves it similarly open to attack. There is also a certain testiness in this vulnerability, as if both

the worker and the agency as a whole do not wish to be reminded of the conflicts inherent in the situation and the dehumanizing effects of the system on them. Staff can thus be overly
sensitive about the reasonableness of recipient demands and
the felt effects on the system as a whole. Even small measures of
welfare rights prodding can be out of proportion to their size.

Some of the same sensitivity was evident in the administration's determined stand against publicity initiated by welfare
rights groups. Many statements were made at different levels
about avoiding public attention to welfare matters triggered by
welfare rights organizations, expediting recipient requests, or
granting concessions to preclude this. Granted that any organization would wish to prevent outside interference and scrutiny
(especially an organization with the fiscal problems of an urban
welfare department), granted also that any public bureaucracy
would want the public to believe that it can handle all of its
problems (especially those relating to its clientele) in a smooth
and efficient manner, there should still not be, on the face of it,
such strong aversion to recipient-sponsored publicity. The administration, after all, would expect neither the public at large
nor office holders to be bothered about or responsive to welfare
rights members' charges that the agency is not oriented to their
needs. The public, as a matter of fact, is more interested in sav-
ing tax money and might very well wonder, as did the supervisor quoted earlier, why these people weren't "using that energy
to find work and get off welfare." The agency would not reasonably expect a surge of prorecipient sentiment in the general
public to be initiated by welfare rights protests. Further,
welfare rights groups do not have enough of a power base to
constitute a serious threat to agency operations. Ehrlich and
Tropman write of the "credible threat" that must be "posed if
the voices of dissent are to be heard by those in positions of
authority." [39] That "credible threat" here derives not so much
from its source, admittedly of little power, as from the impact
it has on a susceptible system. Indeed, the explanation for this

disdain of publicity may very well lie in a general vulnerability. Apparently the system needs to keep outside observers
from the awareness of how inexactly it meets its publicly
avowed, client-oriented goals, and this is part of its overall vulnerability.

The observed dysfunctional responses to welfare rights pressures also illustrate the theme of vulnerability. The dysfunctional response may have much to say about the potential for
institutional responsiveness to the complaints of the clientele,
for those responses seem to be related to vulnerability. Because
vulnerability is built into the welfare system, there will continue to be breeding ground for these and like responses.

The staff member who recounted the reversals of decisions
by upper-echelon supervisors specifically used terms like "vulnerable" and "susceptible" to describe those supervisors' positions vis-à-vis welfare rights pressures. Her implication was that
the supervisors' adaptation to the conflicts inherent in the situation was inconclusive because of their distance from clients;
therefore they were prime targets for the hostile prodding. The
same dynamics could be applied to other personnel, not only
those at some distance from recipients but also others who have
not achieved a modus vivendi regarding the system's tensions
and are similarly affected by recipient pressures. The supervisor's capitulation is only one example of a consequence of a
bind adaptation or lack of it that may occur among various personnel. The issue, of course, is not the individual staff person
but the system's tensions that lead to vulnerability.

The coalitions between staff and recipient groups have also
been seen to lead to dysfunctional outcomes for the system.
Here the specific acts of collaboration that might strengthen
welfare rights organizations or undermine agency procedures
are not in focus. Rather, the emphasis now is on a set of attitudes, held by any politicized worker and acted on by some,
which sees through the system. These workers and supervisors
seem sophisticated about the political source of rules, the need

of the system to control them as well as recipients, and the resultant illogic of many of the procedures. Encompassing generally the "new breed" of workers as well as the unionized workers of varying degrees of militancy, this group holds a different view from that of the traditional assistance worker about the rights of recipients to organize and press demands. By their general posture, they seem to resist the attempts of the system to control and dehumanize them as well as recipients.[40]

Their stance illuminates the special vulnerability of the system to attacks from outside and, more acutely, to inroads from within. Their attitudes and behavior are not only a kind of insult to the system but are also potentially more effective than outside interference. Like welfare rights organizations, their effect is out of proportion to their numbers. There may be questions about the future viability or political course of any particular union or outcomes of interunion conflicts. Whatever the future degree of politicization of staff both in and out of unions, the system continues to be wide open to the insider's exposure of its inherent contradictions.

The organized recipients' challenge that the staff should be accountable to them and not to higher rungs in the system opens another sore point in the situation. In a sense, the recipients are calling the system on its own rhetoric, for officially the institution says it is there to serve people in times of need and to help them constructively out of that crisis. The contradictions in agency functions, which have already been discussed at length, are thus exposed, and the staff is made aware of the conflict between recipient demands and the many structural features in the institution that constrain them to be accountable only upward.

Because of these bureaucratic constraints, the staff members try to control the work situation without interference from organized recipients, in order to pace the immensity of the work and deal with their own particular struggle with the conflicts in the system. As with other professions, they also need to feel in control of the professional aspects of service to clients.

When welfare rights groups bring pressures, the dysfunctional responses may go beyond the practical ones, cited earlier, of interference with caseload management (as the "command to demand" structure implied) to involve encroachments on the areas of accountability and the bind. They do actually interfere with work schedules, but they do more by their pressures. When organized recipients insist the worker follow the rules and thereby grant them all their entitlements, they are holding the worker accountable to them. When they point out that all those entitlements are barely enough to feed, house, and clothe their families, they are forcing the worker to be cognizant of the very real effect of the system's shortcomings. When they refuse a professional interpretation of their problems or, for example, a casework- and not a rule-determined decision about a special-need request, they undermine that aspect of worker control as well.

In a sense, the recipients are insisting on their viewpoint and their definition of the problem. Staff is vulnerable to this approach because the system does not take the recipient's view, although it claims to do so. The staff might be hard put to answer the recipients' challenge as to which side they were on.

Some general inferences can be drawn from the above discussions of dysfunctional responses and vulnerability. The notion of the dysfunctional response was introduced in the previous chapter to characterize those rejoinders to welfare rights demands which disrupted usual agency operations in some way and therefore might point to those outcomes of welfare-rights–agency interactions which in fact represent an appreciable recipient impact. Here, the theme of vulnerability has emphasized a pervasive condition in the welfare structure and a common attribute of the dysfunctional results.

If one were to come to some conclusions and possibly make

some predictions about the overall effect of welfare rights activities, it seems important to repeat first that welfare rights organizations do not constitute a bloc with political power and are unlikely to achieve their ends through that medium. Therefore, it seems more appropriate to focus on the narrower range of making the system more responsive to its demands. There seems to be an association between responses dysfunctional to the system and areas of vulnerability which speak to that question.

On an individual level, the supervisor with a shaky adaptation to the bind is liable to acquiesce to recipient demands. (The prorecipient worker, aware of this in a supervisor, purposely refers his dissatisfied client to that supervisor.) The agency as a whole is vulnerable to a coalition between workers and recipients and to the challenge of the recipient as to its accountability. Both workers and recipients thus demonstrate the system's contradictions. The system is powerless to prevent legitimate exploitation of its rules. All of these areas of vulnerability reflect the basic nature of the system and are potential focuses for challenge.

The arguments made in this chapter about professionalism and vulnerability are all of a piece. The same forces that preclude truly professional behavior also create the system's vulnerability: the contradictions between manifest and latent goals obscure causal factors; those latent goals turn staff members into control agents instead of autonomous practitioners. These contradictions, and other obstacles both to a service orientation and accountability to clients, hamstring the staff, and also produce an institution wide open to criticism.

Another part of this total picture is yet to be stressed. Far from permitting professional behavior amid accountability to recipients, the welfare system dehumanizes its clientele. Crucial to this analysis is the thesis that for every dehumanizing procedure there must be a staff person carrying out the practice, thus dehumanizing herself as well. This can be a disheartening prospect to press into the staff's awareness. The optimistic aspect of this is the parallel property of the exits from this mutually harmful enmeshing—as staff members individualize and humanize clients, they are similarly humanized.

Vail's comments about dehumanization in the welfare system can serve as an apt preface. Having called for a complete revamping of the welfare system, he adds:

> The caseworkers and officials are not to be blamed, except insofar as they may refuse to examine themselves and what they do to dehumanize others. They are trapped also—just as much as the victims they serve. It is important [therefore] that staff constantly examine itself and its practices. But it is of no use for them to become paralyzed by indecision and guilt. Nor does it help to overextend the concept of dehumanization and thereby reach the absurd position that all rules and regulations, all discipline are dehumanizing. Rules and regulations are not per se dehumanizing, indeed they can represent the noblest of man's efforts to control himself and keep the world safe, peaceful and just. It is in the misapplication of rules that dehumanizaton occurs.[41]

The perspectives he offers—of the need for self-examination by the staff and the place of reasonable rules—undergirds this discussion.

It may seem far afield, and too dramatic an extreme an example to employ here, but Goffman's descriptions of the effects of total institutions on the populations they "serve" suggests comparisons to the welfare situation that are not easily dismissed. Goffman's analysis focuses on enclosed and isolated places of residence and work, such as prisons and hospitals. Recipient status obviously does not result in that much encroachment on the person. The recipient is neither confined nor physically separated from her usual surroundings, and much of life continues as before. Yet Goffman suggests that "none of the elements [described] seems peculiar to total institutions," [42] and in a number of crucial ways, the recipient suffers as does the prisoner and the patient. Without being enclosed or isolated, the recipient "takes on a disidentifying role" [43] and institutional procedures can degrade and humiliate him.

Even a few of Goffman's observations suggest analogies to welfare's dehumanizing conditions. Then one is reminded that for every cited practice, there is a representative of the system on the other side of the desk enforcing that procedure.

Consider Goffman's description of the mortification of the new entrant to the total institution, who loses a sense of self and of the enactment of his usual roles, and is now subject to the humiliating procedures of the institution. The degraded status for the welfare recipient, the agency policies which emphasize his inadequacies in not fulfilling the earning role which society prescribes, the sense of powerlessness in the face of procedures he doesn't understand all illustrate that mortification is not restricted to the total institution. The person's entrance, Goffman writes, "is prima facie evidence that one must be the kind of person the institution was set up to handle." [44] In view of society's derogating attitude toward recipients, this may explain why, for example, in Briar's study of new recipients, many reported that they had delayed the application for aid until the last possible moment when all resources were depleted, in order to forestall the humiliation of the application.[45]

Consider Goffman's portrait of "stripping," which in the total institution encompasses a literal relinquishment of every possession—clothes, personal articles and documents, even hair style—as well as the stripping of the person's autonomy: the "violation of one's informational preserve regarding self," [46] and an incursion into the person's "adult executive competency." [47] The parallel is obvious, though in a lesser degree, in the type and amount of personal information required of one in a public-assistance application, in one's submissiveness and dependency on the agency not only for the bare necessities of living but also for direction about one's behavior for fear of being declared ineligible, and, of course, in one's divestment of all but minimum resources. There have been such humiliating practices, to use only one of numerous examples, as the insistence that the recipient deposit his car's license plates with the agency as proof that he will not divert aid granted for living expenses into the car's operating costs.

Of the many "dehumanizing features" of the system which Dumpson lists, three illustrate both mortification and stripping:

> The confiscation of resources and the resultant destruction of incentives essential to sustain self-effort. . . . The established policy of dealing with clients in isolation from representatives of their organizations or from legal counsel, increasing their sense of helplessness and alienation . . . the passive, helpless, insecure childlike role assigned to the client that intensifies his despair and alienation.[48]

Again I would stress that in each instance there is a staff person enforcing the procedures.

Even Goffman's "looping" phenomenon has its counterpart in the welfare system. His definition of looping refers to the lack of protection the inmate or patient has against the possibility that an aspect of his behavior exhibited at one time and in one context may be misused against him in another circumstance within the institution. "An inmate's conduct in one scene of activity is thrown up to him by staff as a comment and check upon his conduct in another context."[49] One has only to scan a few case records at a welfare department—dossiers comprising entries by a series of workers, each of whom might have known the recipient only briefly but many of whom might have commented on the most intimate aspects of the recipient's life—to realize the potential, if not the actuality, of looping. The parallels to Goffman's insights are hardly exhausted, but the point has been made. In his total institutions, and in welfare as a less total one, there are serious reductions of the client's humanity—invasions of privacy, stereotypical thinking, attributions of inadequacy, decreased autonomy and increased dependency—"direct onslaughts upon the self." [50]

Argyris's comment on Goffman's work moves us to the staff side of these interactions:

> Goffman suggests that "inmates" see the "staff" in terms of narrow hostile stereotypes and the staff often see the inmates as bitter, secretive, untrustworthy and lazy. The staff tends to feel superior and righteous, the inmates inferior, weak, blameworthy and guilty.[51]

I have amply argued the reason for society's derogation of the welfare recipient, and have shown the many particular mechanisms by which the institutional procedures accomplish this, as well as the indignities protested by welfare rights groups. How does it happen, though, that staff members will act as agents in these depreciating procedures? What happens to staff in the process?

To examine this phenomenon, Bernard, Ottenberg, and Redl's analysis of dehumanization is exceedingly useful. I shall pursue their argument as it stands, because it seems relevant to the process by which persons come to engage in dehumanizing practices. The authors first make a necessary distinction between self-directed and object-directed dehumanization. The first of these relates to

> self image, and denotes the diminution of an individual's sense of his own humanness; object-directed dehumanization refers to his perceiving others as lacking in those attributes considered to be most human. . . . These two forms of dehumanization are mutually reinforcing; reduction in the fullness of one's feelings for other human beings, whatever the reason for this, impoverishes one's sense of self; any lessening of the humaneness of one's self-image limits one's capacity for relating to others.

. . . In its most complete form object-directed dehumanization
entails a perception of other people as non-human—as statistics, commodities or interchangeable pieces in a vast "numbers
game" . . . together with a sense of non-involvement in the actual or foreseeable vicissitudes of others.[52]

The authors acknowledge that there may be some degree
of adaptive dehumanization—"some appropriate detachment
from full emotional responsiveness"—so that the task at hand
will not be impeded. (Many professionals who serve others
know that there are times when some cushioning and distanc-
ing are necessary.) The authors next proceed to describe mala-
daptive dehumanization and some overlapping aspects of its dynamics. These are, in a sense, an interlocking series of causes
and effects in an individual's dehumanizing behavior.

1. Increased emotional distance from other human beings.
. . . One stops identifying with others or seeing them as essentially similar to oneself in basic human qualities. Relationships
to others become stereotyped, rigid and above all, unexpressive
of mutuality.

2. Diminished sense of personal responsibility for the consequences of one's actions. . . . One "safe" way of dealing with
such painful feelings is to focus only on one's fragmented job
and ignore its many ramifications.

3. Increasing involvement with procedural problems to the
detriment of human needs. There is overconcern with details of
procedures, with impersonal deindividualized regulations, and
with the formal structure of a practice, all of which result in
shrinking the ability or willingness to personalize one's actions
in the interests of individual human needs or special differences.

4. Inability to oppose dominant group attitudes or pressures
. . . [it is] more and more difficult to place [oneself] in opposition to the huge pressures of the "Organization."

5. Feelings of personal helplessness and estrangement.[53]

I would be repeating major portions of the welfare rights
study were I to attempt to document the many parallels be-

tween this process as Bernard and her colleagues have so perceptively outlined, and the corroborative instances in the welfare system. The result is what has been termed "people-work —a nightmare epitome of man as an inanimate object." [54]

The suggestions that have been made within the social work profession that workers must somehow reconcile the attacks by the institution on the client's integrity with their own professional values distorts the issue,[55] and in fact, as Briar suggests, raises a false one.[56] The worker's protection of the client's civil rights (a necessary condition for the enhancement of his humanity) must take precedence in service to the client, Briar insists, and in fact should be in no inherent conflict with professional values. I would add to the argument here that the protecting of the client's humanity protects the worker's as well. "Captor-captive states," Wineman and James observe, "are inherently inimical to the human condition for they jeopardize the humanity of both captor and captive." [57]

Clarifying the incongruity of professional service in the same setting in which civil rights are violated serves not only the purposes of questioning the reconciliation of these two phenomena and of affirming that the reconciliation may only obscure the dehumanizing practices, but also the possibility that even imposing rehabilitative services on a welfare recipient has its own dehumanizing aspects—less blatant as they are than many other welfare procedures. "There is a real danger," Freidson writes,

> of a new tyranny which sincerely expresses itself in the language of humanitarianism. . . . I believe that in imposing one's own notion of good on others one always does the harm of reducing their humanity.[58]

One is reminded of the attribution of individual responsibility for dependency status and the concomitant imposition of casework services. For reasons not related to what is really in the interests of their autonomy and integrity, people can be misused by a social institution such as the welfare system, even under the guise of professionalism.

I have pressed this hard look at the dehumanizing practices of the welfare institution, to emphasize particularly that these practices envelop both client and worker. But it fortunately follows that any changes that permit staff members to treat recipients with more humanity enlarges the worker's humanity as well. The dehumanization process is a reversible one.

Again, Bernard and her colleagues:

> A reaction of massive indifference—not hostility—leads to grievous cruelty, yet all the while, in another compartment of the self, the same individual's capacity for active caring continues, at least for those within his immediate orbit. . . . As we strive to distinguish more clearly among the complex determinants of adaptive-maladaptive, humanized-dehumanized polarities of behavior, we recognize that stubborn impulses toward individuation are intertwined with the dehumanizing trends on which we have focused.[59]

These "stubborn impulses toward individuation"—the humane concern for others—are, of course, what make the bind the dilemma that it is. Perhaps the greatest impact that welfare rights groups make is to activate the staff's humanity. Lipsky speaks, in the context of protest politics, of the need for powerless groups to activate third parties with power—e.g. the mass media, powerful interst groups—in order to bolster their protest.[60] The third party that welfare rights groups activate may very well be the staff's latent "stubborn impulses toward individuation." I have attempted to press the point that it is in the staff's best interest as well to permit and encourage this activation.

Dumpson writes:

> The only honest thing for "regimented bureaucrats" to do is to recognize that the chains that bind us are the same chains that bind the destitute and the poverty-stricken; that there is consid-

erable invalidity in our methods and structures; and that as the chains are unbound we should leap forward to seek better, more valid ways.[61]

Each of the three issues discussed in this chapter—professionalism, vulnerability, and dehumanization—have been ones brought to greater clarity by the pressures of welfare rights organizations. Welfare rights groups have surfaced the issue of professionalism, by their charges that the welfare system is not accountable to its clientele but to another public, and that professionals have been misused by the system. They have exposed the vulnerability of the system, its contradictions, and its susceptibility to pressure, notwithstanding its capacity for countermeasures. They have laid open to view dehumanizing practices, as, in contrast to other recipients, they have evolved a different definition of themselves and have insisted on their civil rights and personal integrity. These discussions have built on what the welfare-rights–staff interaction has revealed, and in turn they underlie the considerations in the chapter to follow. There, the effort will be made to specify other models for professional behavior—in Dumpson's terms, better, more valid ways—suggested by the welfare rights experience, which will make the system less contradictory and less vulnerable (at the same time, exploiting the vulnerability that does exist), and that will hopefully result in greater humanity for both the servers and the served.

CHAPTER SEVEN

Change Strategies

The connection between the findings and the issues of previous chapters and the strategies of this one is a more than logical one. Hopefully, it will have direct practical implications as well. If the issues brought into focus by welfare rights pressures have served a clarifying purpose; if the portrayal here of the nature of the bind, the latent purpose of the welfare system which dehumanizes both client and staff, and the constraints on professional behavior make sense to those involved, then such awareness in and of itself can act as an impetus to change. Welfare rights prodding is meant to be unsettling and to initiate a certain dissatisfaction with the way things are. Further, if these issues have been conceptually well-grounded, if they make theoretical sense as well, they should also serve to determine the kind of changes to be made. If one understands that the welfare system is dehumanizing to all concerned, one may then seek ways to reverse the process. If professionalism in this kind of people-serving bureaucracy is cast in a different light, the search would then be for conditions that allow for a truer professionalism. But to discuss how an institution like a welfare bureaucracy can be humanized involves the difficult task of translating the impetus for change into some soundly based strategies.

First, I need to discuss some issues involved in making the leap, in an organizational setting, from the conception of needed change to specific tactics for change. That discussion has the more important purpose of providing a base not only for the tactics considered here but also for other, potentially more useful, ideas about strategies that might later evolve.

IMPLICATIONS OF LINE-WORKER FOCUS

Both the strategies and their associated areas of organizational knowledge will center on workers in the lower echelons of the welfare agency, those with most direct contact with clients: the line workers and their immediate supervisors. This study examines most carefully these interpersonal encounters of welfare rights members with social workers, and sometimes their supervisors, although welfare rights pressures are brought at higher levels within the agency. This lower level is where the bind is most evident and it is also where much of the legitimation of welfare rights groups occurs. Further, this focus on line workers reflects the basic stance of welfare rights activities: changes can be initiated at the lowest tier of this pyramidal structure. Extension of that focus to strategies of change considers how efforts toward humanization within the institution can similarly be initiated within the lower ranks.

It is not my intent, however, to limit my audience to the line workers. The problems addressed by the strategy considerations are those which other staffs may also experience—the management of the bind (being in the middle between client and organization), maintaining a professional posture in face of organizational imperatives, attempting to humanize services.

Because the focus is on welfare's lower echelons, any change strategies in which they might engage need to be viewed within two perspectives: the place of their change efforts in the context of other avenues needed for institutional change and the potential effectiveness of the lower echelons of organizations.

What impact they can reasonably expect to make places some practical boundaries around humanization efforts.

Strategies for change focused on social work staff need first to be placed in the perspective of the array of needed change in the welfare system. The major causative factors for the numbers of the assisted poor and for the nature of the system serving them lie outside the control of social work staff. The exits from the present sorry situation depend on, in the broadest sense, social and economic policies that provide constructive jobs for those who can work and an adequate income maintenance program, based on right, for those who cannot. National programs of this kind would be of the greatest consequence in meeting the problems of the poor and humanizing the welfare system. As such policies are unlikely to be effected in the foreseeable future, other approaches available through alternative governmental sources might eventuate in some shifts in policies. Supreme Court rulings—e.g., removal of residence requirements, nullification of the "man-in-the-house" policies— and lower-level court procedures, can help to humanize the welfare system. Liberalized administrative changes at the Federal and state level can have impact on programs in operation in local departments.[1] Outside pressure groups with some community power might press for client-oriented changes. Administrators of local welfare agencies, concerned with staff morale and effectiveness, may use professional consultation services to humanize the system, at least for staff members.

Each of the above is conceived to be essentially outside the control of line workers and supervisors. This is not to say that workers can have no impact on any of these possible alternatives; as politically active citizens they can help to effect these modifications. Rather it is to say that such remedies are out of the reach of lower-echelon staff. With that array of needed recourse for change and in the light of the significant lack of impact to date of any one combination of these on the overall welfare problem, it may seem that anything an individual or small group of workers can do would be singularly unimpressive. However, this array is meant to place staff efforts in some realistic proportion to others, but clearly, not to negate those efforts. My argument is that humanization efforts, at even the lowest levels, can have ripple effects throughout the system. Later discussion of strategies will provide some basis to test out that argument.

Further, the focus is on change specifically initiated by line workers. There is much in the literature on how higher administration or outside consultants may affect organization change,[2] as well as commentary on how evolutionary forces within society, e.g. technological advances, bring organizational shifts in their wake.[3] Here the attention is on the impetus coming from line workers, and so a relevant question concerns the likelihood of success from that quarter. There may be more potential effectiveness from those sources than is commonly assumed.

Beyond the general awareness that lower level groups do in fact modify institutional relationships [4] there have been some perceptive insights about the unexpected power of lower-echelon staff. For example, Mechanic examines the "source of power of lower participants in complex organizations" and finds a number of successful avenues.[5] Because they have some specialized expertise, a readiness to exert effort and interest, a knowledge of rules (and of how to exploit or circumvent them), and crucial access to "information," persons, and instrumentalities (e.g. equipment), staff members at the lower levels do indeed exercise considerable control over the actual functioning of the organization. The power does not derive from the formal role structure but rather evolves from the staff's use of various informal mechanisms. There is no implication in Mechanic's analysis that individuals engage in such practices other than for the protection or enhancement of their own positions or others in coalition with them, but the potential for humanization purposes is there. Mechanic's point is simply that the means are effective.

As another example, Cressey found that even in a regulation-bound institution such as a prison, there are limits to the controls from above placed over the prison guards. Though he is the lowest level worker in the organization, the guard must also be considered a manager of the inmates in his charge; "because he is a manager, his activities cannot be bureaucratized in a set of routine procedures." [6] He thus must be given some discretion. In fact, it is recognized that guards must be free to violate certain rules in order to prevent both inmate dissatisfaction and potential prison disorders. Therefore the guard is not a mere rule follower but has some degree of power over the actual functioning of the institution. This phenomenon will be seen to have some parallel to strategies focused on the relationship between the welfare worker and his client.

To these suggested areas of power of subordinate staff, I would add the special circumstances here of the vulnerability of the welfare institution. Previous discussion of the system's sensitivity to public confrontation about its inherent contradictions adds a further dimension to the possibility of effectiveness of staff of whatever level.

As comment on the immediate future, separation of the administration of services and eligibility has the prospect of an intensification of conditions that make for the system's vulnerability and for the bind. Many more untrained staff members will be confronted with client needs they cannot meet, and professionally trained workers can be expected to have heightened dilemmas about their appropriate roles.

However, even if workers are not deterred by the realistic limits on results of their efforts, and are in fact even encouraged by the potential of lower-level activities, a number of personal forces may operate to prevent much rocking of the boat. Staff members may have vested interests in the status quo for reasons of economic security, while supervisory personnel may wish to retain their particular niche in the bureaucratic power structure. Brager's exhortation that "professional employees in an expanding and understaffed field can afford to take more risks than many have been willing to" may be less well grounded in periods, such as the immediate present, of diminished opportunities for social work positions.[7] Still, at any time and for personal reasons, action aimed at institutional change may not be a part of an individual's usual repertoire of behaviors, and as Jaques observed in his study of industrial change, "continuing with a problem was considered to be less painful than undergoing the changes required for its resolution."[8]

Strategies for change useful to staff members must take into account a variety of individual predilections toward such behavior. Howard and Somers's insightful commentary on the diversity of roles individuals can play in their attempt to resist "institutional evil from within" speaks to such personal predispositions.[9] Their typology encompasses the active and passive role, the visible and invisible actor, the person acting alone or in concert with others, as well as the timing of action as a variable. Though they stress the relative utility of some of these several variations over others, one is impressed with the choices available. Choice of strategy may vary, and the actor is not cemented to a particular role. Those supervisors earlier described as having engaged in a "palace revolt"—i.e. pressuring the agency to change personnel policy—may, at another time and in another context, be quite administration oriented.[10]

Recognizing that there can be considerable staff resistance to action toward change based on individual concerns (one's personal position, one's view of what is acceptable professionally, constraints about what one can comfortably draw upon from a repertoire of individual or group behaviors) it may still be mentally unhealthy to be passive. There should not be a prescribed set of actions to achieve humanization, because the statements above emphasize individual choice. Also, there should not be a kind of alienated militancy. In fact, a certain balanced attachment to the organization may be essential. The warning that "complete commitment to the organization will not promote innovation . . . [and] neither will complete alienation" reflects that stance.[11] But autonomous actions, sensitive to the client's humanity, can yield the important by-product of improving the work situation for the workers themselves. (That this may also be a way out of the bind for staff is a further advantage.)

Societal attitudes toward the assisted poor require a work organization that will carefully control the actions of the system's functionaries. The system's rules are meant to delimit staff behavior as much as that of the client. The results in organizational terms resemble what has been described as the negative effect of the "mechanistic" organization, where decision making and control come entirely from the top and dependency and passive conformity are expected of the staff. These effects can be a stifling of the worker's abilities, a subservience to superiors, a waning sense of responsibility. In reaction to pressures from above, the employee resorts to a number of "adaptive antagonistic devices," [12] including among others absenteeism and—the welfare system's particular albatross—turnover, aggression, and alienation.

This reference to the effects of a mechanistic model of organizations, as discussed by Argyris and others, is not meant to imply that the source of the problem for staff is the type of organization found in the welfare system. Clearly, societal attitudes constitute the basic source. Furthermore, it is not my intention to imply that a mechanistic model in a service organization is necessarily dehumanizing to staff and client. The example of the Social Security Administration is a case in point. The difference, of course, between the Social Security and the public welfare systems is in the striking contrast in societal attitudes toward the recipients of service. This contrast leads to differing staff conditions.

The extent to which workers are not passive, the extent to

which they can engage in purposeful humanizing efforts—as for example the mutually supportive and prorecipient activities to be suggested shortly—is the extent to which they transform their own work situation. Workers can create oases of independent behavior even within the limitations of a controlling hierarchical institution, permitting somewhat more creative possibilities for themselves. It is of more than incidental interest that by demanding to be viewed and treated as autonomous individuals, welfare rights groups are indirectly pressing staff toward intraorganizational behaviors beneficial to the workers themselves.

Some strategies, descriptions of which follow, build upon a set of assumptions: that there are staff members who wish to take a more active role toward humanization; that the evidence for the potential of lower-level staff is suggestive enough to be tested further; that greater autonomy and self-enhancement is healthier for both staff and clients; that a number of personal forces means careful attention to the risks to be taken; that there will be a variety of individual dispositions to actions and a legitimation of even small steps. Finally, though the role of the social work professions to humanize the welfare system has some realistic limitations, it is not conceived to be without possibilities. Consider Thompson and McEwen's statement about related institutions:

> It was not public clamor that originated revisions in public school curricula and training methods; the impetus came largely from professional specialists in or on the periphery of education. The shift in focus from custody to therapy in mental hospitals derives largely from the urging of professionals, and the same can be said of prisons. In both cases the public anger, aroused by crusaders and muck-rakers might have been soothed by more humane methods of custody. Current attempts to revitalize the liberal arts curriculum of colleges and universities and technical institutes have developed more in response to the activities of professional specialists than from public urging.[13]

The greater involvement of the public welfare professional in similar transformations seems worth the effort.

STRATEGIES FOR HUMANIZATION

The strategies to be considered are ones that have evolved specifically from the staff–welfare-rights interaction. They are, therefore, only a part of a total configuration of humanizing changes that might be implemented in the public welfare system. They are focused primarily on what individual personnel or informal groups of staff might do within the ordinary range of their activities. These strategies therefore do not encompass other change activities that would be more broadly conceived, perhaps more systematically analyzed as to sources of power and tactics of action systems. And although they are also staff-inspired, they are related to institutional changes beyond those changes tied to welfare rights pressures.[14] The strategies described here do stretch the traditional boundaries of staff activities and are meant to be responsive to welfare rights demands in a conceptual sense—e.g. recognizing the value of strengthened recipient groups and a different definition of the individual recipient. In this sense, strategies limited to welfare rights issues would not be unduly restrictive. For, if staff could effect even some of the client-oriented modifications welfare rights groups demand, the system would have gone a long way toward humanization. And along the way, not insignificantly, the staff would have humanized the organization for themselves as well.

First of all, staff members could take a series of actions to bolster and extend welfare rights groups. These actions would not only be taken because of the staff's increased acceptance of clients' rights to organize themselves (although it is sometimes too easy to give lip service to that not entirely unimportant notion), but also, more significantly, for the service orientation advocated here. Thus action to strengthen the groups would be seen as a means by which recipients could press for accountability to themselves. That accountability is an attribute of professional behavior that is sorely lacking in the welfare system. There would thus be a conscious recognition that the organized recipients' pressure to have staff answerable to them is a push in a healthy direction, and a push that requires clamor from below. This would mean seeing welfare rights organizations in a favorable light, instead of as a kind of additional nuisance implied by the complaint of a supervisor that such organizations added to the organizational stresses to which she was already subjected, or as an insult to the professional competence of those staff members who maintain that client dissatisfactions should be resolved in a context of casework. The first step necessary is to see welfare rights as a constructive force, one that may upset the status quo for the staff, but one that might help to bring social work in public welfare to the client-oriented position that it should maintain.

These specific tactics could be described as the aforementioned "creeping legitimation," now made conscious and purposeful. This can be as simple (and as profound) as referring clients as often as possible to welfare rights groups. This can be done by an individual staff person—an eligibility or a services worker, one trained or untrained, and either of the line or the supervisory staff. It would mean making explicit and extending a number of staff actions found in the study, many of which indicated the utility of welfare rights groups to staff.

Clients can be referred for a variety of reasons: to enable them to know the full extent of their rights and entitlements; for help in clarifying an issue of eligibility; for the therapeutic benefits of association with others who share common problems. Each of these reasons aids the worker in the management of her caseload. For that same reason, staff members may turn directly to welfare rights groups for information on rules and procedures about which recipient members may be more knowledgeable than they. Staff members may, in addition, refer clients especially to strengthen the recipient's position vis-à-vis the system, for welfare rights help in pressing a claim, for welfare rights representation at fair hearings,[15] to encourage altered and more self-respecting definitions of themselves in their roles as recipients. Even the suggested attendance of a recipient at a meeting of a government body at which welfare rights groups press their point of view can assist in this last purpose.

Welfare rights organizers are aware that recipients are often reluctant to join the groups because they are hesitant to acknowledge their recipiency status in public or because they fear that their membership will lead to the discontinuance of aid. When staff members actively refer clients to welfare rights groups for whatever reason, they help to dispel both these hesitancies.

In addition to serving the staff's immediate goals, these referrals accomplish a further purpose. The more the groups are used and the greater the membership grows, the greater both their strength and legitimation. The utility of welfare rights groups to staff was an unexpected finding in the study. I am suggesting that these purposes be more consciously exploited and extended in order to enhance the groups' legitimation. A significant advantage to this heightened legitimacy and strength is that these are advances which the welfare system cannot rescind in the same manner that other countermeasures can be instituted. It cannot rule against the uses which the groups serve for both clients and staff.

The risks for staff in this process vis-à-vis the system would seem to be limited. As long as the agency administration accepts the existence of welfare rights groups as legitimate, they might be hard put to prevent staff referrals. Some agencies, of course, have gone much farther than the one studied toward incorporation of welfare rights activities within the agency structure. Some have, for example, provided office space for welfare rights personnel. Granted the possibility of rulings, as found in this agency, denying workers the right to meet with groups of recipients on agency premises, individual referrals are nevertheless not likely to be countermanded. The greater risk might be the one illustrated in the contradictory statement cited earlier about the staff's voluntary referrals of clients mixed with fear of the organized recipients' subsequent behavior to the referring staff. It is possible however that the latter eventuality might be dealt with differently. In the earlier comments relating to staff's appraisal of the legitimacy of welfare rights demands, it was noted that staff members questioned such legitimacy if they believed that recipient participation in such protest groups was incongruous, if they preferred a casework resolution to the recipient's complaint, or if they feared that recipients might want considerable changes in the system. Should staff members assume a modified position on any or all of these counts, it might be easier to dispel the recipients' personal hostility by not questioning their basic right to confront the system. This was illustrated by several union members who worked in coalition with recipient groups, but who refused to accept overt hostility personally addressed to them. With such an acknowledgement of their basic claims but with a rejection of unfounded personal animosity, the result could be more adult and reasonable behavior on all sides.

This matter of support and use of welfare rights groups is not without official sanction. Among the suggestions for client participation made by the Department of Health, Education and Welfare to welfare agencies throughout the country have been 1) to encourage organizations of recipients who are strong enough to represent themselves; 2) to develop methods of carrying on a dialogue between administrative heads of departments and organizations of the poor for response to questions and complaints and for interpretation of needs; 3) to encourage participation of recipients and other poor people in hearings and on study and advisory committees.[16]

Such administration-initiated actions are not to be depreciated since they too can lead to strengthening and legitimation. They also have the disturbing tendency, though, to result in co-optation and cooling out of the recipient groups. The uses of welfare rights groups for staff members, especially if on an individual and reciprocal basis, are not so likely to lead to co-optation. A sense of partnership would also be more apt to develop in these relationships as both staff members and recipients see themselves as caught in the same dehumanizing net.

One of the obstacles to professional behavior toward clients in public welfare is the lack of accountability to them as the beneficiaries of the system. Strengthening and legitimating recipient organizations is one way for the groups to be encouraged to act as a constant reminder to staff members of where their primary responsibility lies. Further, the reason for the lack of accountability is intrinsically tied to society's definition of welfare recipients as degraded nonpersons, responsible for their dependency. Strategies that aim at a different definition can also help to modify some of the distorted bases of the system. One of these tactics has just been discussed—the definition of the recipient as a person with a right to organize group confrontations of the system. Other measures to evolve a different definition of the recipient can be instituted, directly within the context of the worker-client relationship.

The literature reflects an apparent dichotomy between working with individuals and modifying social institutions. For example Wiener urges that group workers carry on their work along with, but separate from, action to effect change in the social system.[17] My argument for a closer meshing of the two functions is meant neither to deny the importance of social action taken by professional and citizen groups aimed at vitally needed changes in social institutions nor to obscure the requirement that professional behaviors be enlarged to include the required activities to press for these organizational changes.[18] None of these actions, separate from the worker-client relationship, is in any way minimized by my focus.

However I do argue here that if, as the welfare rights groups demand, the public welfare staff redefines the recipient's role, the staff can bring about institutional change. Let me illustrate: in the course of the study, several workers stated that they had a different relationship with those clients who were welfare rights members than with others in their caseloads. The welfare rights member presented herself as a person with a right to aid, who was knowledgeable about the system, who did not see the worker as someone offering her personal rehabilitation services. Therefore, she saw the worker as an agent who would make certain that she would receive all her entitlements rather than as a therapist. Some workers were annoyed with this alteration of traditional relationships; others welcomed the change. If increasing numbers of staff members approach their clients in the way that welfare rights members demand, then the character of the welfare system must change accordingly. If workers come to view their clients as rights-bearing citizens whose dependency problem is essentially a socially caused one, there would then be some impact on the latent purpose of the institution, which sees the client as a suppliant in need of rehabilitation. If the worker assumes the role of agent instead of therapist, and attempts to secure for the recipient all her available entitlements (using welfare rights groups as sources of information about these) rather than to rehabilitate a personally defective recipient, then the basic nature of client-serving shifts. Granted that much modification of worker roles would be required to make an appreciable impact, a challenge to the institution's latent purpose and to the way services are administered can nevertheless have ramifications throughout the system. The analogy with Nonet's study of the workman's compensation agency again comes to mind as an example of a changed institution resulting from a changed conception of the client and his problem. These possible modifications would also be illustrative of the "power of lower participants in complex organizations," and would in addition indicate how the institution can be humanized for staff members, as their roles are enhanced through autonomous thinking and acting about organizational tasks. Further, it would dispel the notion of an inherent dilemma, of a choice to be made between services to individuals and organizational change efforts. They can occur simultaneously.

This revised definition does not call so much for specific staff tactics—as in the suggestion above for welfare rights referrals —as it calls for a different model of staff-client relationships and of what might be expected within this changed paradigm. Two models that can serve as foci here and be considered as alternates to the agent-of-the-system–therapist dichotomy are those of broker and advocate. Briar's description of the rationale for each can then lead to what can be gleaned from each for use in these considerations:

> The justification for this function [that of social broker] resides in the fact that there are many persons who need services but do not know that these services are available; many others who know that the services are available but do not know where to obtain them; others who know where to obtain services but do not know how to get them or else face obstacles in seeking and obtaining them; and still others do not know how to gain the maximum benefits available to them. . . . Increasingly, if a person is to gain from these agencies the benefits to which he is entitled, he requires an informed and skilled guide who knows the social welfare maze, knows the bureaucracy, and knows how to move it to get what the client needs and deserves.[19]

The advocacy role constitutes more of a challenge to institutions. Briar continues:

> Currently, we are being told by lawyers, who at last are becoming interested in social welfare problems in sufficient numbers to make a difference, that performance of the advocacy function by social workers is essential both for the client to get what he is entitled to receive and for the social welfare system to operate as it is supposed to, especially as it becomes more institutionalized. . . . Many of the persons whom caseworkers

seek to serve, especially among the poor, will not exercise their rights, press their claims and needs, or appeal actions that adversely affect them unless someone performs the role of advocate, because many of the clients are too apathetic, feel too powerless, or are too uninformed to do so. Moreover, effective performance of the advocacy function would help to insure that agencies are attentive and responsive to the needs and desires of clients. . . . If case-workers act upon these principles, they will find themselves challenging the policies and operations of established organizations and institutions of the community, including—in some cases—their own agencies.[20]

The contrast between the two roles—that of broker and that of advocate—not only clarifies what is characteristic of each but also makes evident that the advocacy role is the more difficult and risky for the worker.[21] Still, each focuses on certain characteristics of the people served and of the institutions that serve them. These characteristics can, in turn, change the welfare worker's role. Certain propositions might then be developed as a basis for strategies, for example, that 1) clients of public assistance agencies cannot be expected to understand the network of this and other institutions and that social workers can come to see that their expertise should be available exclusively to serve client interests; and 2) welfare agencies are not designed to meet client needs adequately and do in fact engage in many degrading and frequently illegal practices so that to have a more proclient stance involves the assumption that the institution is the adversary, or at the very least that the client is not assumed to be the target for change.

This is not to imply that a worker in public welfare can blithely act on these ideas (if convinced by them) as if he were a private entrepreneur, though obviously he has more leeway to be a broker than an advocate.[22] But it does mean that, within the point of view forming the basis of these two roles, he can define the recipient and her position vis-à-vis the institution very differently. He can seek ways for his activities to approximate the broker or advocate stance and he can act on a belief that is common to both—a belief that he is there to serve his client's interests, which are often disregarded by the organization. Further, the worker can engage in such specific acts as the referral to clients for welfare rights representation at fair hearings so that the advocate role, if not performed by him, at least is available to the client. And it is not incidental to add that the extent to which the worker can act as his client's agent as she makes her way through the system—or against the system if necessary—is the extent to which he is relieved of the pressures of the bind.

Two important outcomes may very well ensue if the worker acts upon a transformed definition of the client and of his own role in relation to the client. The first is that the client may very well alter her conception of herself and her behavior. Experiences of mental patients whom staff members expected to discharge,[23] or others assuming task roles,[24] and that of school children expected to exhibit spurts in learning abilities [25] serve to confirm the proposition that individuals respond to what is expected of them. It is relevant to stress here that in the instances just cited the individuals responded differently because the professionals involved anticipated that they would do so. And if we are concerned with where a welfare worker's expectations might lead, it is also relevant to add that the model of the welfare recipient as an autonomous individual with confidence in her rights, rejecting both moral judgment or unrequested rehabilitation, is a more humanized person than the confused suppliant at the mercy of the institution.

The second outcome is that the worker, by treating the client within a different framework and having a more independent client confronting her, will be less apt to engage in dehumanizing practices. Client and worker interests in this transformed view can be assumed to be the same—what humanizes one humanizes the other. In sum, some approximation of the broker and/or advocate model (more akin to the legal model) [26] on which strategies can be based in individual work with clients has more to recommend it in this situation than the disease model which, as elaborated earlier, has been misused by the public welfare system. A redefinition of the role of the welfare recipient is more likely to occur within the former.

Beyond the uses and legitimation of welfare rights groups and the values of a revised definition of the recipient, the study findings also suggest the humanizing potential of cohesive groups of workers and particularly of their coalitions with recipients. In the agency examined these were unionized workers, but the idea to be advanced here is that there might be a conscious exploitation of groupings of staff members, whether unionized or not, to enhance the service orientation toward clients. Apart from any individual staff person's decision to join a union, there might be still available to her—and to clients—the advantages of cohesion and coalition that the unions showed. I propose a combination of insights from organizational writings about the importance and utility of informal groups with the observation in this study of their use in humanizing both clients and workers. The two strands coalesce to suggest certain strategies.

The importance of informal groups in organizational life was alluded to earlier. Students of organizations stress that the personal satisfaction from cohesive primary groups, the value of autonomous task forces, the group as a medium for change, the productiveness resulting from positive emotional involvement with fellow workers [27] are all crucial elements in the internal processes of organizations. Add to these two observations touching closely on the central issues here: that social workers have tended to be more colleague-oriented than client-oriented [28] and that mutual reinforcement from like-minded colleagues can do much to maintain a proclient stand against dehumanizing odds.[29] The strategies now take these ideas one step further and suggest putting to purposeful, proclient use the groupings that form naturally and are of such importance in the staff's work life. The observations of union activity in the study suggest that, beyond what further political purposes unions might serve and the controversies that surround these, and beyond the personal benefits sought by the unionized staff, the notions of cohesion and coalition in the service of the client can be built upon by nonunionized personnel as well.[30]

First of all there are significant sources of mutual support that groups can afford their members. In attempts to look at, analyze, and take seriously, ideas about initiating specific action toward humanization, however small in dimension, the reinforcement of trusted colleagues cannot be overestimated. The forces against client-oriented activities are considerable and courage gleaned from others is a crucial counterbalancing element.

Both the exchange of ideas and the planning of activities are of value within informal groups. Such strategies as those already presented—for the increased use of welfare rights groups and for the evolution of a transformed definition of the recipient within the worker-client interaction—could now be put on the "agenda" of groups of workers, so that these efforts could be made in concert.

Coalitions of groups of workers and organized clients enhance the humanizing efforts of both. The degree and structure of a group's involvement in such alliances is a flexible matter. The union–welfare-rights coalition is one model. There could be others. Even though such coalitions may vary in structure, effectiveness, and longevity,[31] they signify that the humanizing interests of clients and workers converge, and this may be as important as the specific results. And to weave in earlier threads of this book's arguments, these alliances both exploit the system's vulnerability and add to the power of lower echelons.

Finally, a set of strategies can be tied to the system's voluminous rules by using them for humanizing purposes. Turning rules to those purposes involves certain stances toward both recipient and the procedures. This means a belief in the recipient's right to know and have accessible to her the rules that delineate her entitlements. Welfare rights groups insist on this availability and worker-recipient coalitions have been used, and can continue to be used, to make manuals of procedures and other rule information readily obtainable by recipients. This means also an acceptance of the principle, based on the recommended redefined view of the recipient, that rules should be used to the hilt to provide as much as possible in grants and services to recipients. Though it is a formidable job to attempt a thorough knowledge of mountainous packages of policies and procedures, the greater the worker's awareness of the existing rules, the greater the possibility of exploiting them for the client's benefit. Mention was made earlier of an intake worker who searched intensively for rules to declare applicants eligible. Though his exhaustive but successful effort is not feasible for daily practice, his experience is an instructive one regarding the possibilities that do exist to work the system for the client's benefit.[32]

Strategies based on rules can also be derived from an understanding of both their manifest and latent purposes. The avowed aim of the welfare rules—procedures related to human service leading to healthy independence—can sometimes be exploited by finding and adhering to those rules which reflect that purpose. The ruling related to an educational trust fund, reported in the study, is a case in point. Howard and Somers note that

> even in authoritarian agencies like the police force, members dedicated to humanitarian values may successfully invoke the protection of the book.[33]

These men seek out and emphasize to fellow policemen those accepted procedures which are less likely than others to lead to dehumanizing practices, and by calling on those moderate rules they meet the "expectations of a legalistic role and get others to conform to the humanitarian book."[34] This selective use is, of course, based on extensive awareness of what rules are available. Following from this, another use of informal groups in welfare agencies might be to apportion among the members the overwhelming task of knowing which among the many rules that exist can be exploited to achieve the group's manifest purpose.

Vail's experience in trying to humanize a mental hospital is applicable here. With the aid of nurses new to the institution, certain dehumanizing practices were identified and substitute procedures initiated.[35] Though these changes had the full support of the hospital's administration and so were easily instituted, the paradigm of the search and implementation might be imitated, at least in part. If, again through staff groups, dehumanizing practices could be brought into focus (dehumanizing aspects of rules can often be blurred with constant use) then choices can be made about the use or modification of available procedures in order to approximate a humanized goal.

I have contended that the latent purpose of the rules is to control workers as well as clients. If this idea has credence, then the impetus to use rules fully and to humanize procedures for clients may be intensified as staff members see that they too will be humanized.

Each of these strategies has been built upon some relevant conceptual understanding. Accountability to the client in a service organization is an imperative for professional behavior, and so tactics are proposed to encourage the strength and legitimacy of welfare rights groups who insist on that accountability. Society's traditional and degrading definition of the welfare recipient has rationalized many dehumanizing practices. Strategies to transform that definition would therefore seem necessary. Both staff and clients are conceived to be caught in the same dehumanizing process and coalitions between them seem to be a way out for both. Rules similarly constrain them both and selective use of the rules for humanizing can be, in like manner, mutually beneficial.

This relationship between strategic and conceptual elements is emphasized, so that the strategies can be seen to have a theoretical base and so that this handful of specific strategies may hopefully be enlarged as additional tactics are spawned from these sets of ideas. Restricting strategies to those prompted by the welfare rights study also serves to stress the potential of the consumer's voice in institutional change. The strategies have, in addition, been purposely limited to those entailing a minimum degree of personal risk to staff. This seemed to be the potentially most useful approach, and to address a broad spectrum of staff members.[36]

Seeing the conceptual logic in such ideas as those grounding the strategies advanced here and of their feasibility as tactics is, for social work staff, only the first step toward their actual implementation. Succeeding steps come harder. Added to personal reluctance to disturb the status quo, there has been much in the professionalization of the social worker that precludes such actions. As Patti and Resnick argue, social workers have lacked "both the tools and the formal professional support" to seek institutional change. Furthermore, as others have also emphasized, social workers are educated to avoid conflict and to value consensus. Of particular importance here, workers are also instructed to place loyalty to the agency above service to the client.[37] Encouraging social work staff to engage in the kind of strategies developed here means an appreciable change in their professional identity. That shift comes when both the educational process and the professional supports stress the primary responsibility to the client. Such accountability helps to insure that client needs are met; the focus on the staff is in no way meant to obscure the overriding concern for those unmet needs. Additionally, the accountability enhances and humanizes both the worker's professional self and her place of work.

CHAPTER EIGHT

Humanizing Other Institutions

When any institution's clients challenge the nature of its services, one can expect that this will put to a severe test the knowledge base and service orientation of the professionals whom the institution employs. Those demands for accountability are also apt to reveal the latent purpose of the organization, as well as its dehumanizing practices, and thus will highlight the bind that professionals experience. However, client activities not only force a keen appreciation of the bind but they also go further, and by example show that change can be initiated from below. The overarching ideas with wider applicability are, then, that client demands highlight the elements of the professional dilemma, and further, that lower-echelon staff members can extend the client's example and take action to extricate themselves from the bind—and of course by so doing give better service to their clients.[1]

Beyond these general ideas, certain specific aspects of service organizations, as revealed in the welfare-rights–staff interaction, overlap with the properties of other social institutions, and so some of the theoretical issues developed from the welfare interaction may be common to many other circumstances. In this way, the present study may have specific expanded usefulness. The intent of these discussions is neither to superimpose the analysis of welfare onto other situations nor, as will be evident below, to analyze systematically other social situations along each of the dimensions illustrated earlier. Rather, a sampling of issues will be used to test for comparability to and difference from other social institutions. This brief overview of commonalities and differences can hopefully assist others to determine what they can use from this study, and what they will add from further inquiries, to arrive at workable strategies for humanization.

Dehumanization in people-serving organizations is perhaps most likely to occur in those institutions whose clientele is overrepresented by the poor and nonwhite [2] and, as Beck and Ryan [3] among others would testify, this is not by accident. We blame the victims of faulty economic policies and of racism, and the institutions established to solve the resultant problem —clinics for the poor, public housing, prisons, welfare agencies —reflect that distorted reasoning. Yet the concern for humanization ranges farther and has gained momentum in recent years, as the white and nonpoor have joined the dissatisfied and have registered complaints about such issues as schools and universities, the delivery of medical services, and urban-renewal programs. Their charge is that institutions are not working for their clientele as they should be doing, and like the organized welfare recipient, clients insist on accountability to them.

Though such confrontations sometimes involve the top administration of the institution or policymaking governmental bodies, the focus here will remain, as in the welfare instance, on the working professional—the teacher in the slum school, the clinic doctor, the university professor, the urban planner. This focus continues because this is where the challenging encounter has its most personal impact and, even when made elsewhere, where the clients' complaints can have exacerbating effects on the dilemma professionals inevitably experience between human needs and organizational constraints. Furthermore, this continued focus will once more stress the potential power of lower echelons in a people-serving organization.

As some corollaries are now drawn between the welfare situation and those of other institutions, the focal point is on the staff professional and in particular two facets of the challenge made to him: that his professionalism is being called into question and, further, that the person challenged works in an organization, and one governed in the final analysis by societal imperatives.

CHALLENGES TO PROFESSIONAL AUTONOMY

To begin with, there are marked implications for the concept of professional autonomy when clients "no longer accept uncritically the service offerings of the establishment." [4] Much as the welfare worker uses a therapeutic stance to withstand client challenges, professionals in other settings have long been steeped in the protection afforded by their statuses and so recoil at the client's attempted incursions. Freidson's discussion of the self-defense mechanisms in the medical profession is perhaps the most carefully drawn portrait of the process [5] but, of course, the brittle professional posture is endemic. For example, writing of the urban renewal situation, Seaver notes that

> sometimes when the community begins to ask hard questions, professionals retire behind a mantle of experience and qualifications to demand that their judgment be accepted as the revealed truth.[6]

Or, in observing community pressure on the slum school, Janowitz stresses the effective exclusion of parents from normal educational planning and adds: "Basically, the slum school officials, because of their defensive posture, see the intrusion from the outside as potentially disruptive." [7]

A first step toward humanization is a willingness to become aware of practices that have been shielded by a hardened professional attitude. A cherished professional attribute has been that of autonomy—to decide what the client needs and to administer service without lay interference—and admitting the client into these sacred precincts goes against the grain. Of course, considerable autonomy will continue to be a requisite for professional practice,[8] but a more precise look at the specific challenges to professional autonomy may place the client's attempted inroads and the professional's reaction in some balanced perspective. The crucial issue may center not on autonomy per se but on reasonable boundaries to its exercise.

Disputes over limitations on professional sovereignty made in other settings seem to echo the questions raised earlier about the professional's inadequate base of knowledge and his limited service orientation.

> The articulate poor charge that the middle-class ghetto teacher is blind to their particular problems, does not understand their children, is ignorant of black history and innovative teaching methods.[9]

Gans's study of Boston's East End is testimony to the lack of knowledge displayed by urban planners about the meaning of the community to its displaced residents.[10] The claim is made in contemporary medical planning that community demands for a broadened scope in medical care require a very differently trained physician.

> Preventive care, early diagnosis, and rehabilitation are the new demands. They cannot be met by traditional hospital-bound medical practice oriented to acute illness or by physicians whose training echoes the limitations of such practice.[11]

Even in conventional patient care, the doctor, with his scientific aura, is challenged on the basis of restricted expertise. Freidson alleges that the "ideological emphasis on the importance of first-hand, individual experience" is "directly contrary to the emphasis in science on shared knowledge, collected and tested on the basis of methods meant to overcome the deficien-

cies of individual experience."[12] Added to this are the inadequacies in the accessibility of medical services and the varying
definitions of medical problems—different for the patient and
for the medical establishment—so that there is no valid estimate of the nature and extent of many disease entities. Friedson once more:

> Should the profession define an illness by signs or symptoms
> that the general population considers to be trivial and unim-
> portant, or shameful or stigmatized, the profession's conception
> of that disease is likely to be distorted and partial, resting on
> highly limited knowledge of and experience with its attributes,
> and on inadequate statistics of incidence, prevalence and signif-
> icance. In such cases, the practitioner is less informed and less
> qualified to evaluate the "illness" than are those who are able
> to go into the community and study the behaviors and re-
> sponses that actually take place.[13]

The evidence mounts that there is both a misreading and a
deficiency in the informational foundation of many professional services, and it is on the basis of relevant, esoteric knowledge that society grants both autonomy and special status.

In addition, there are any number of circumstances similar
to those in the welfare system, when societal and organizational
constraints preclude a viable service orientation to the client.
Even in the most rehabilitation-oriented prison, the prison official must, first of all, prevent inmate revolts, for he knows that
he has a vulturelike press and an unsympathetic public waiting
in the wings, prepared to exploit any disorder.[14] The revealing
differentiation that Krause makes between the two publics to
which urban renewal officials address themselves indicates the
violation of commitment to those whom the programs are intended to serve. The "cliental" are community interest groups
who will benefit from urban rehabilitation; the "target" groups
are the poor of the central city who, far from benefiting, find
themselves arbitrarily displaced.[15] The teachers in slum schools
are caught up in the school board's need to report academic

achievement in its school population, despite the fact that such competition prevents adequate attention to the children's special learning needs. The university faculty is acutely aware that outbreaks of student dissatisfaction, many validly grounded, may have a harmful impact on relations with the board of regents or the legislature. Even in that singular province of the doctor-patient encounter, seemingly less tainted than any of the above by societal constraints, and in which the doctor's humane concern is supposedly sacrosanct, the medical profession has "less and less come to reflect what the public asks of it and more and more come to assert what the public should get from it." [16]

A moral evaluation of the client is a further facet of institutional attitudes toward the clientele of service organizations that very much colors professional behavior. This has been amply demonstrated in the case of the welfare system and is obvious as well for the prison inmate. Other examples, although not so apparent, nevertheless indicate that through a certain definition of the client (similar to the welfare recipient's degraded status and supposed need for rehabilitation) intrusions by practitioners have been rationalized. The hospital patient is defined as dependent and childlike, and in some facilities staff members have assumed management of patients' social security and welfare income. Indignant patients charge that the medical profession has "no license to handle patient finances as well as their physical needs." [17] Schools in impoverished areas adopt a mental health model toward the neighborhood families and

> assume that the resources of the family of the slum are so limited and its values so at variance with the goals of the school that the school must seek to become responsible for the total social space of the child.[18]

University students were characterized as less than adult and amid claims that the university stands *in loco parentis,* control over many areas of students' personal living conditions had been justified.

"When decisions are at bottom moral or evaluative rather than substantive," Friedson claims, "laymen have as much if not more to contribute to them as have experts." [19] Freidson's argument goes further in claiming that many of the definitions physicians ascribe to disease entities and many decisions made about patient managements involve moral evaluations and encroachments on civil rights—areas far beyond professional competence. He is writing in the context of the medical profession, but the limits he places on the expansion of autonomy could very well apply to each of the above. The essence of these instances is that clients say that they are themselves qualified to determine the limits of the practitioner's management of their "case." Haug and Sussman believe that there is evident in the current "client revolt" the demand of the "right to define the problem and then call upon the specialist in a narrow domain." [20]

More systematic analyses of each of the instances cited through these commentaries on professionalism would reveal crucial differences from those earlier specified for the welfare system. The particular lacks or distortions of practitioners' theoretical understanding, the specific way in which the service orientation is dulled would vary, each from the other. What they share in common with the circumstances in public welfare is that the professionals involved may not have all the relevant facts, do not put their clients' (or patients' or students') interest foremost, and may make a moral evaluation that can distort service. These conditions permit neither individuation nor respectful treatment or humanization of the person served.

ORGANIZATIONAL ISSUES

Also analogous to welfare conditions is that the workers function within organizational settings, and thus the factors associated with such conditions come into play. As argued above, even in an organization heavy with constraints, staff members can seek specific and allowable tactics to humanize client service.

There are significant variations, however, in how organizations serve clients. These variations limit extrapolation from the welfare situation. Many service organizations deal with inpatient societies, some to them captive, and as writers on prisons and mental hospitals observe, unique forces—such as patient and inmate subcultures—are set in motion there, diverse from the state of affairs when clients are not totally within the social space of the organizaton.[21] These can have major impact on the course of events within those walls—an impact that should not be underestimated in comprehending the texture of organizational life there. However, some of the comments made about the "society of captives" in prisons indicate that the rules seem to have much of the same characteristics as those in welfare—the bounds on staff as well as prisoners, the problematic nature of both interpretation and adherence by the enforcers.[22]

The format of client service will vary but the lesson from welfare about the gap between the institution's manifest and latent purposes finds corollaries elsewhere. The characteristics of these contrasting purposes will be peculiar to the particular situation, but if one is concerned with humanizing services, the latent purpose may be the one to watch. Pious words may be said about urban renewal for the poor, treatment for the prisoner, the development of an inquiring mind for the university student. But the realities also include the rehabilitation of the inner city for the well-to-do rather than for the poor, the overriding imperative for inmate custody and control of prison disorder, the insistence that the graduate become an informed but not rebellious member of the establishment. In each instance, the professional is trapped in a vise created by the contradictions between the two goals.

Hardly coincidental is the convenience of defining clients in such a way as to rationalize the latent purpose. The process was argued fully in the case of welfare. The references made just above to the moral evaluations of the client are of the same mold. The characterizations of the client may exhibit varying degrees of personal slur, but each is used to justify the moral superiority and superordinate position of the practitioner. The teachers of the slum schools believe that the parents are "incompetent and ineffectual in helping to educate their youngsters."[23] In other school settings as well, the parent is defined as "unpredictable and uncontrollable."[24] University students are viewed as nonparticipants, lacking in a sense of responsibility for the academic enterprise. The doctor approaches his patient at the very least in a patronizing manner—as one unable to evaluate his own problem, or with few rights over its management—and at worse, in a contemptuous fashion.[25] The slum dweller is assumed to be inevitably the destroyer of property,[26] and the public housing tenant shares much of the moral stigma of the welfare recipient.[27] The parolee is defined as a potential threat to the community, so that in probation work the rights of the community rather than those of the former inmate are to be protected.[28]

The societal and institutional definitions—the evaluative handiwork of those whom Becker terms "the moral entrepreneurs"—justify, in turn and ironically, the practitioner's stance and institutional strategies to control this man-made deviance.[29] Vinter's analysis of treatment organizations suggests that this process is clearly seen in "people-changing institutions"—for example, correctional and mental institutions—whose designs are "calculated to result in relinquishment of nonconformist patterns of conduct, disapproved values and deviant identification."[30] However, with the slum school in mind, even in the "socializing institution" (Vinter's other category), moral judgment and the correction of deviance can be very much part of the picture.

CONTRASTS AND COROLLARIES

In the analogy drawn so far between the welfare system and other people-serving organizations where dehumanization is an issue, I have attempted to show, through a sampling of such institutions, both parallels with and departures from the circumstances in welfare. I have made specific references to professional issues that surface when humanizing efforts are to be addressed (matters of professional autonomy, knowledge base, and service orientation) and to organizational questions, particularly those of structure of services and the achievement of the organization's latent purpose. The emphasis both on similarities and differences has been made to invite the use of the welfare example where suitable, but to urge the individual study of each institution, if viable, for the development of appropriate strategies for humanization. That same argument holds in those situations where, as in public welfare, clients have protested their treatment at the hands of the institution. There as elsewhere, demanding processes require a careful scrutiny, because they may hold keys, as they did here, to choices of tactics. Separate analysis is invited because it cannot be assumed that demands made by clients of other organizations will trigger the same sequences of events or expose the same factors as those resulting from welfare rights protests. Each situation has its special circumstances.

Several examples may strengthen the point. A most likely comparison to welfare rights organizations would seem to be Community Action Programs. These are indeed organizations of poor people, of those previously not organized, impatient for altered power relationships with social institutions, and confronting these institutions abrasively. But shortly the two situations diverge. Community Action Programs set out to organize a diversity of poor people—not only recipients who share a common problem and a common stigma, but also the unassisted poor who are differently defined. Though the role of the unassisted poor as participants may be awkward and unusual, their status is not a degraded one. The multiplicity of Community Action Programs' institutional targets dilute the sense that one set of clients is grappling with one institution. Further, the

Community Action Programs received official, not welfare rights, sponsorship; thus the programs' leaders became arbiters rather than advocates.[31]

Residents of public housing who organize tenants' strikes, groups of parents who seek local control of their school systems, students who protest against universities, all share with welfare rights organizations the commonality of a clientele making demands on social institutions. Still, a tenants' strike is the sort of weapon welfare rights groups do not have, and in the two school situations those protesters can, by boycott and sit-in and strike, effectively shut down the target institutions, a possibility not open to recipients.[32] As a further point of difference, the status of the university undergraduate or parents of school-age children is hardly a degraded one. A model for confrontation by students urges their "recognition that they are an underclass,"[33] hardly an exhortation required for the recipient.

Only careful inquiries into the interactions ensuing from each of these and like protests, as played out in their own special circumstances, will indicate whether these are the differences of consequences (and the only differences of note) between other demanding interactions and the welfare rights situation.

However, two aspects of the impact of client protests might be expected to appear, no matter what other variations ensue. The first aspect is the client demand for a redefinition of his status vis-à-vis the institution. Indeed, the act of protesting itself forces a redefinition. The call for a "physician-person dyad" to replace a traditional "physician-patient dyad"[34] and the insistence that the low-income person contribute to rather than be excluded from her child's education are examples of such demands. The second aspect is that client challenges will inevitably exacerbate the bind experienced by the practitioner caught in the middle. Krause's comments on the protest by the poor against urban renewal illustrate this consequence. They force into the open the detrimental effects of the program and contrast them starkly with official pronouncements about benefits accruing to the poor. Here as elsewhere the pull between the client and the organization, between manifest and latent purposes, squeezes the professional.[35]

Exits from that dilemma can be forged from varied materials and, similar to the welfare instance, they are not wholly the responsibility of those practitioners who form the lower echelons of large social institutions. In each illustration used above, as is true for public welfare, there are a number of available approaches to humanization: legislation and other governmental measures, community pressure groups, the impact from professional associations, and so on. But if the focus is on the organization's practitioners, as is true here, then the strategies for change are of a special character, to be evolved from a thorough analysis of the possibilities within that institution.

I do not offer that kind of analysis here, but only the example of welfare as illustrative of possible strategies. Some of the potential and problems noted in other institutions, however, can be seen to parallel the strategy considerations in the welfare system. Specific tactics appear in other places, either naturally formed or purposely created. For instance, coalitions exist between prisoners and guards in which the inmates are humanized through bonds of friendship, where rules are bent or ignored, and where the notion of the power of lower echelons finds some backing. Coalitions can be constructed by those not usually in partnership. In the Mobilization for Youth experience, teachers were encouraged to "stand with the poor against their own superiors." [36] New definitions of clients can be created, as illustrated by a patient-operated project in a mental hospital, involving real and meaningful tasks, which emphasized the patients' work potential rather than their illness.[37] Task groups in hospitals—where nurses often serve as team members—may be a more natural environment for the utilization of informal groups in humanization efforts than would be true for the teacher, for example, who tends to be a lone performer. The complaint registered about the lack of professional guidance for the probation worker caught in the trap between his professional training and the punitive system around him [38] is but one example, akin to the arguments made earlier of the need for wider professional support if practitioners' humanization attempts are to be successful.

I did not claim in the welfare discussions that the strategies offered exhausted the possibilities, and I certainly make none here that these brief remarks even touch the surface of factors relevant to humanizing devices in other people-serving organizations. Indeed, the premise underlying all of the corollaries to other institutions is that only from a thorough understanding of theoretical issues and practical considerations in each particular instance will humanizing strategies for that institution evolve. My study of the welfare system uses one possible model for such analysis.

CHAPTER NINE

Conclusions

It will be obvious to many in the public welfare field, as it is apparent from the many references cited here, that the faults of the system—the components of the bind as I have outlined them—are nothing new. For the handful of writers who were sharply critical long before welfare rights organizations appeared on the scene, the deficiencies of this institution were all too apparent. For many other observers, awareness of the inequities was not far below the surface. For those who work in the system, that awareness, sharper for some than for others, has also been close at hand. Many of the staff members have recognized—at least tacitly—that the system dehumanizes everyone it touches, that therapeutic services in this milieu are not the answer to a problem of this sort and of this magnitude, and that as staff members they have been placed in an intolerable vise. Welfare rights pressures simply—and profoundly—act as a catalyst, to crystallize and expose the elements of the system that have been blurred for some by rhetoric.

For the practitioner, the effect of the organized recipient is to undermine the jargon about the institution's purpose. The client's bold assertions cannot be sidestepped, for the staff has no solid ground of a service orientation to fall back upon. And so there is an insistence that the reality be faced, which forces into the open hitherto ignored facets of the system. For the outside observer of the process initiated by welfare rights pressures, there is a parallel consequence. Just as the groups press the practitioner toward a more sobering and transformed view of the system, the effects of their demands enable the observer to assemble varied commentaries in this institution, many previously offered, some emanating afresh from this interaction— about the system's conflicting purposes, its network of rules, its lack of client orientation, and so on—and to construct an analytic view that may be more closely aligned with reality. As one experiences these client pressures or studies their consequences, their crystallizing capabilities become evident. This is the effect of the process upon the book itself, which I wished to stress: that whatever clarity has eventuated about the essential nature of the system and what might be done to alleviate its dehumanizing influences is a direct result of the capacity of client protests to act as a catalyst.

It may very well be that, as challenges made to other people-serving organizations are studied, this same phenomenon will be manifest. The complaints of clients, as compared with professional dissatisfactions, have a special quality. Practitioners or academicians can deplore an institution's contradictions and chafe against its constraints on clients and themselves, but there seems to be a qualitative difference when organized clients do the same. Perhaps it is because their stance takes even concerned practitioners out of the realm of coffee-break discussions or agendas of professional meetings, and brings them in confrontation with those who are affected so harmfully by the system and know why this is so. Perhaps it is because these are not merely a set of individually hostile clients but groups who are concerned for others as well as themselves and who are knowledgeable about how the institution affects them all. It is one thing for a social worker to face an angry client who complains about her personal situation alone; it is another to be confronted with a group constituted to press the class case and prepared to elaborate on the deficiencies of the entire system, in which staff is also enmeshed. In any event, client input provides a singular spurt to the cause of humanization. For not only does the staff then conjecture about and commiserate intellectually with the miseries of the client, but these ills are presented, with no protective veneer, by the people themselves, and with their insight into the dehumanization of the staff as well. And it is the argument of this book that a careful look at the consequences of such demanding processes may furnish a more forthright comprehension of what's wrong with people-serving institutions and perhaps in addition some ideas about how to change what's wrong—essential steps toward humanization. This seemed to be so for the welfare system and may be true for other client protests.

In the welfare instance, the impact on the system occurred along several dimensions. First, until their advent, "the social welfare apparatus had always had its own way with the poor." [1] The practices questioned by organized recipients could continue to exist (and to a great extent still do) because recipients do not believe, as welfare rights members now do, that they are rights-bearing citizens and that one of these rights lies in questioning the operation of the system itself. The institution cannot have quite its own way as before.

Secondly, their pressures constitute a moral criticism—"An appeal to the authority of principles in support of one's view" [2] —and such a basis for demands can be exceptionally effective here, because the system presents a contradictory face to the world and abiding by moral principles is not one of its noteworthy attributes. Welfare rights can thereby place a number of issues in bold relief: that the rules are not there for equity but for maipulative control; that procedures are sensitive, as equitable rules should not be, to shifting political pressures; that the many layers of agency operations show only disdain for the system's beneficiaries. Their moral criticism illuminates to the staff the vise they are in and taunts their lack of adherence to the principles they officially avow.

Finally, their presence precipitates a loss of usual controls in this rule-applying institution teeming with restrictions. The theme of vulnerability indicated how tenuous that control can be, despite the inches-thick manual. For what the system cannot hold in check, despite the mountain of constraints, is the potential in the staff for seeing through the system, out to the recipient.

Then, when the recipients bring pressure to bear, these several forces are set in motion. The client is now an active participant, insisting not only on rights, but on a transformation of long-standing relationships. Many of the staff's customary reconciliations of the contradictory imperatives of the system—to assist but barely and with contempt, to watch every move but somehow to encourage trust as well (reconciliations that consider the institution and not the client)—can no longer work in quite the same way when recipients call them on their officially stated commitments. The loosening of usual controls extends to the establishment of worker-recipient alignments which result in a far greater threat to the agency than the conflict-ridden worker or the occasional defector to a prorecipient view. The agency can stiffen bureaucratic measures to retain control but it cannot in fact restrict the welfare rights' use of rules for its own benefit, the legitimation accruing to them as cooptation ensues, or the unique services welfare rights groups can offer its members and the welfare staff. It also cannot control the vulnerability of the system itself.

These consequences of welfare rights demands offer a conceptual understanding of a contemporary phenomenon, with some potential parallels to similar occurrences in other institutions. As such, this analysis may provide insights into an important social process, and through additional studies in other settings a body of theoretical knowledge may accumulate about the course of events set in motion when clients dispute the claims and practices of service organizations. Further, even this one process may hopefully provide fertile ground for the development of ideas for institutional change so that the prospects for humanization may be enhanced. An attempt was made here to do that, by building upon ideas derived from the observed interaction for the development of specific strategies.

One might say that a certain philosophy, one that goes beyond concrete tactics evolving from the consequences of welfare rights demands, was copied from the welfare rights experience. Their model asserted that attempts to transform the system could be undertaken by those assumed to be powerless. If one can conjecture about the interpersonal effects of the groups on their own members—and even without careful study this does not seem far-fetched—there is both a paradigm for action and a close tie to knowledge about humanized organizational life. For one could expect that as recipients become active in their groups, they become more humanized—that is, they develop a sense of control over their circumstances, become knowledgeable and assertive instead of powerless, and can function autonomously instead of submissively. These are precisely the properties recommended for the role of a more humanized employee of any organization.

The observations gleaned from the welfare rights study may also have relevance to efforts to transform the system from without. Earlier, a program of income maintenance to replace the public assistance system was cited as a major route to humanization of service to the poor. The focus on staff action within the institution did not specifically encompass attempts to bring about those revisions, and in fact the premise of the strategies was that the system was unlikely to be basically altered in the near future. What is worthy of some discussion however is that the basic rationale of this system—clarified by the demanding process and forming constraints on staff's humanizing efforts—can also be clearly seen to impede efforts to transform the system.

Thus, in considering alternative income maintenance programs to substitute for public assistance, the essence of the welfare system continues to dog designs for change. In focus here are not the many technical considerations pro and con on various proposals but the parallel of their common dilemmas with the factors in the bind. When proponents of Children's Allowance or Negative Income Tax or other measures contend with matters such as incentives to work, break-even levels, assistance to the working poor and the nonpoor, they are in the heart of societal attitudes toward the assisted poor—the attitudes that help to create the bind.[3] What may be economically feasible and more effective in the long run is a different sort of question—of costs and benefits but resolvable on another level —from the concerns about what is politically feasible. Political acceptability can be translated to mean what the general public will permit to be granted out of its tax money to poor people, just because they are in need and with no strings attached. Attitudes of hostility toward and derogation of the assisted poor put serious obstacles in the way of future programs and are precisely the ones that contribute to the present bind.

Advocates of income maintenance plans stress the advantages of universal coverage so that no stigma will be attached to beneficiaries, yet the public may not be willing to abandon the imprint. The same planners are concerned about particular features that might affect incentives to work. Though there are both commentary[4] and current experiments[5] which might indicate that an income floor does not adversely affect the spur to work, the public may continue to be reluctant to take a chance on a group whose motivations it does not trust. There are serious concerns among planners about meeting the dual imperative of an adequate basic income and a reasonable total cost, but the nonpoor may be averse to accept either that level of adequacy or the cost to them.

The strength of these societal attitudes—common both to future considerations and the present welfare system—needs no further documentation than the difficulties involved in trying to effect some form of guaranteed annual income at an adequate level of assistance and the deleterious effects on recipients and staff of the existing welfare institution.

A corrollary to this view is that income-maintenance programs that continue to retain a means test in any form will also be encumbered with the trappings of the present system. These place staff members in a severe bind, preclude professional services, and make the system vulnerable to welfare rights pressure. Until there can be a break from the traditional, there will be an uphill fight against the pathologies of this particular bureaucracy. Admonitions, as from an HEW official that "it is extremely important that welfare recipients begin to feel that the welfare worker is on their side instead of on the side of the agency," [6] are hollow ones. A structure based on the means test and control of the worker and client mitigates against that alignment. It may be only within coalitions based on the client-oriented framework outlined earlier that the recipient will know, without exhortation, where the workers' commitments are directed. Incrementalism in welfare revisions may be all that is politically possible (and the arguments above would certainly support that view) but it will carry in its wake a heavy burden of bureaucratic constraints. Perhaps a contribution of the welfare-rights study is a somewhat sharper portrayal of those constraints.

If one could imagine a very different picture—universal income maintenance at an adequate level, a set of competent social services available to all, a stress on the advocacy role of the social worker—the issues at the core of this study would be only of historical interest. Anything less than that requires administrative discretion on eligibility. Again, imagining a situation without present societal pressures, these determinations might be made by social workers more accountable to recipients than to antirecipient claims of the agency. This could be likened to the present Social Security Administration, which advertises its program, encourages and supports beneficiaries in the establishment of their full entitlements, and makes no assumptions about the psychosocial problems of its clientele. It is not administrative leeway itself that is harmful, for as Jones writes,

> it is not possible to draft effective legislation in many regulatory and welfare areas without leaving leeway for the exercise of administrative judgment and rule-making and adjudication.[7]

Instead, political and societal interests make of that administrative mechanism a tool of control for both recipient and staff.

It may take a contemporary version—though hopefully a less devastating one—of the Depression era of the 1930s for the needed transformation to occur. The Social Security programs became acceptable then because it was clearly evident that something was seriously wrong with the country as a whole. Even more benign circumstances can have a similar effect, such as the overriding political and economic concerns in the Canadian experience, which permitted the establishment of a program of children's allowances. In both instances, the individual poor family did not bear the onus of its poverty and the feared consequences of the program did not materialize.[8] Without such contingencies, planners must contend with existing attitudes and conditions, intensified in the current scene and particularly in the AFDC program by the close ties between social attitudes toward welfare and racism.

Significant developments elsewhere attack the problem from another position, which reflects an altered definition of welfare dependency. These are the legal landmarks that chip away at firmly held beliefs and bring rights in the welfare area into the family of other rights—the ideas embodied in Reich's "New Property" [9] and court decisions enlarging recipient rights and restricting administrative controls. In a sense, these overrule societal prejudices and superimpose legal imperatives onto political ones. They can be expected to continue to do so, perhaps tilling the soil slowly for the acceptance of a universal income maintenance system. In a manner akin to the by-products of legitimation for the welfare rights groups found in this inquiry, the legal progress is made in spite of impressive counterforces.

Within the welfare structure itself, the process delineated here speaks to the question of income maintenance alternatives in two ways: it suggests that the same societal imperatives which define the special character of the bind and the controlling rules of the present welfare system also define the obstacles to future alternatives, and it suggests that any income maintenance program which retains the antirecipient elements of the present system will spawn the familiar set of institutional contradictions and a demanding process to exploit them. Short of a major overhaul, administrative mechanisms effective in breaking this sorry cycle might be those, comparable to the legal advances, which somehow can be justified on other than traditional bases. An example might be the general adoption of the application-by-declaration procedure now in effect in many aid programs and which can be rationalized on the grounds of efficiency alone.

The mechanisms the welfare-rights–staff encounters have suggested are of another order. These change efforts would come from the lower tiers of the welfare structure and would not derive from a legislative or administrative power base. Rather than being crippled by attitudes which derogate the recipient, the aim of these change strategies is to modify some of the basic attributes of the system—to devise a different definition of the client and the cause of her dependency, to act upon an altered view of professionalism in this context, to engage in a purposeful struggle against the institution's dehumanizing features.

Howard and Somers advise that in humanization efforts the participants must "disengage themselves enough from the system to gain perspective while involving themselves enough to be effective." [10] My intent has been to provide that perspective to staff—about the elements which comprise the dilemma they experience and about a misused professionalism. The premise has been that a conceptual grasp of these factors precedes and informs specific tactics. Then the effectiveness that might ensue from involvement can be tied to a sense of commitment and some designs for action, to help the staff make its way out of a dehumanizing labyrinth. Thus, both the intellectual perspective and the functional strategy have been stressed. The welfare rights groups themselves offer an example of those at the bottom of a hierarchy, with increased comprehension of the essence of the system, acting on the assumption that change can come from below. The extent to which welfare rights pressures in and of themselves result in the institution's greater responsiveness remains problematic. My thesis has been that one answer lies in what the staff does with the process that the groups have initiated.

This social institution is, of course, not the only one that disregards the full humanity of its clientele, nor is it the only one being challenged by them. The interplay of client demands and institutional responses has been made apparent for the welfare instance, and suggestions for humanization there have been advanced. Whether these can find utility elsewhere waits upon other inquiries. There is a singular contribution to be made by the client toward his own humanization and that of the individuals whom society appoints to serve him. Careful scrutiny of that client input is highly recommended; it may very well give an institution's staff some directional bearings on an exit from a dehumanizing situation that engulfs them all.

Appendix on Method

As any researcher will report, the road to a completed study can be, if not rough, at least circuitous. In a formal sense, the reader is interested in the formulation of the problem as well as in other research decisions along the way. But less formally, I think that behind-the-scenes histories can have refreshing effects on the social research field. This appendix pays respect to Hammond's collection of such research chronicles and proceeds in that spirit.[1]

HISTORY OF A RESEARCH PROBLEM

Frustration, sometimes serendipity, can combine with logic and principles of research in the sequence of research events. My interest in welfare rights organizations developed several years ago from the unlikely source of a sampling problem. In a project concerned with families new to welfare recipiency status,[2] we were stymied in our efforts to secure a sample of recipients who had never received aid before and that accurately reflected the ethnic distribution of the community. We spent weeks trying to locate Chicano applicants who had not previously received aid. Finally, to reach the ethnic balance we wanted, we decided to include a small number of Chicano families who had been recipients intermittently for many years. They turned out to be an unexpected asset to the study. Our interest was in the experience of new recipients in dealing with the welfare system, and the Chicano families provided us with a surprising point of contrast. The families in the major sample mirrored the stereotyped view of welfare recipients as lazy and immoral, spoke of recipients as "they" and not "we," and were compliant in their encounters with the agency. By contrast, the Chicano families showed assertiveness about themselves as recipients, a willingness to acknowledge their recipient status openly, and a protectiveness of themselves and other recipients.

I then became interested in the other end of this continuum of acceptance of the recipient role—the welfare rights member —and in the role changes involved as a recipient joins and continues participation in a welfare rights organization. The larger interest was in the notion of the recipient as a rights-bearing citizen and in the question of how the traditional role of passive recipient is transformed as the person enters into the welfare rights milieu. Later on, as this study has amply illustrated, that concern extended to the question of whether organized recipients, with a rights-bearing stance, can elicit a greater responsiveness from the welfare institution.

For a period of time, my intention was to study role change among welfare rights members and I planned a period as a participant observer among several groups. A number of factors converged to veer the research toward the agency. There was the question of the long-term contribution of the study of welfare recipients as compared with one focused on the welfare system. With interest centered on institutional responsiveness, the latter began to have more to recommend it. Also, the findings of a study of these fledgling organizations might in some way be misused to their detriment—an outcome in which I did not wish to participate. Further, as mentioned in the introduction, there was a growing conviction that the public welfare profession needed to look more honestly at its role in the widely acknowledged welfare crisis. The outcome of the study has only added to this conviction.

The shift from one focus to another appears more calm and reasoned than it was in actuality. Some time and much rethinking were involved in resolving what seemed at that time to be a dilemma about relinquishing a prorecipient viewpoint to adopt that of the welfare agency staff. That dilemma, well represented by the exchange of views by Becker and Gouldner [3] was resolved as it became clear that the conflict was illusory—both the staff's and the recipient's behavior are governed by the requirements of the institution, and any prorecipient change frees the staff as well as the recipient. Further, the symbolic interactionist view which formed my own stance leads to an understanding of each actor's definition of his own situation. In the instance of the public welfare staff, as has been obvious throughout the considerations of the bind, through that view we do not "degrade their [the staff members'] humanity but sensitize ourselves to it." [4]

THEORY AND METHOD

The interactionist view and the exploratory nature of the study resulted in the decision to employ a participant observer approach, or some necessary modification of it. This method would be useful in permitting an openness to a process unstudied previously and in encouraging an understanding of the perspectives of the participants. I planned to observe staff–welfare-rights interactions and other intra-agency events connected with them. Along with interviews with the staff involved, these observations were to be the primary sources of data, for at the outset I expected to concentrate primarily on welfare-rights–agency encounters.

One of the advantages of the research method chosen is its flexibility in reformulating both problem and data collection methods as one proceeds. It soon became necessary to exploit that flexibility. I discovered shortly that specific interactions of welfare rights and staff happened unpredictably as did any staff meetings or worker-supervisor discussions concerned with them. Out of the resultant frustration and in order then to be on hand at the agency when they did occur and to be there in a natural way, I arranged to attend other, regular meetings. What was initially a strategy to meet the original research design became, very soon and very logically, a different framework for the study. I justified my request for observing other intra-agency meetings on the basis of wanting to understand welfare rights pressures in the context of ordinary agency pressures. After observing just a few meetings, the maneuver changed to a logical rationale. What had developed was comparable to Liebow's "natural fit." In his instance, he viewed a group of black men in their roles as "breadwinner, father, husband, lover, and friend" [5] and believed that the "natural fit" of his framework to the subject had evolved because this was much the same way the men looked at themselves. Indeed, as confirmed throughout the inquiry, staff members did not see how else I would fully appreciate the outcomes of welfare-rights–agency interchanges, and especially the staff's role, except through a thorough grasp of the basic nature of the agency and the implications of the institution's constraints on them. I found myself in a situation analogous to Whyte's shift in focus in his study of a neighborhood gang—"Instead of bowling in order to be able to observe something else, I should have been bowling in order to observe bowling." [6]

Other aspects of interactionist theory—the actor's definition and intervening variables, the sensitizing concept, as well explicated in Blumer's discussion[7]—also framed the research. Thus, the independent variable—the welfare rights pressure—was seen to be reacted to by the staff in the context of the rules and other agency requirements, of their adaptation to the bind, and of their appraisals of the legitimacy and reasonableness of demands. The result was the range of responses, the dependent variable. The notion of the sensitizing concept permitted a leeway that proved fruitful. At the outset, for example, I had expected that individual staff would by and large either favor or oppose welfare rights groups and that their responses would be limited to either a granting or a denial of demands. An approach based on concepts limited to that view would have missed much valuable data, for it was soon evident that a contradiction in orientations could exist in the same individual. For example, one worker referred a client because she had a legitimate claim but was at the same time angered by the organized recipient's hostile assertiveness. As a matter of fact, on a few occasions when I asked for the clarification of the apparent contradiction, the puzzled looks and the sloughing off of my remarks indicated that what was incongruous to me was not so to the staff. Also, as fully discussed in the report, the responses encompassed far more than mere denial or acquiescence. I had not anticipated, for example, that welfare rights groups would serve the staff's purposes. Following the initial mention of this, I became alert in subsequent discussions to variations on this theme.

It seemed, in these and many like examples, that the method and the theoretical ideas that informed it encouraged an open and sensitive look at the phenomenon under study and allowed for the development of hypotheses.

SOURCES OF DATA

The department selected for the study is in a metropolitan area in which welfare rights groups had been active for several years. In the negotiations for entry to do the study, there was some initial apprehension that my presence might be in some way exploited by the coalition described in the report and result in further disruptions to the agency.[8] This concern (fortunately short-lived) constituted not just an item to be mentioned in the history of the research but further evidence for the theme of vulnerability.

Data gathering was completed over a six-month period with

observations and interviews both at the agency and in the community. I observed many of the weekly meetings of the administrators of the AFDC division and other meetings, directed by the division head, attended by all AFDC workers and supervisors. All of these were concerned with current operations as well as the impending conversion to separation of services and eligibility. I sat in on several regular conferences of senior supervisory staff and their immediate subordinates, unit supervisors. There are more than forty AFDC units in this agency, each of which consists of a supervisor and five or six workers. I met with most of the units. Some supervisors declined to participate because of work pressures, particularly around the impending conversion. A few said that workload demands, especially uncovered caseloads caused by staff shortages, precluded any regular meetings with their workers. As data gathering neared completion, there was much repetition in accounts of welfare rights interactions and attitudes expressed about them and I believe I had obtained a good approximation of their full range. (Some workers had no personal experiences to report, but still expressed attitudes.) In view of the many work pressures, I was continually surprised and appreciative of the staff's willingness to take the time for this research. For many, of course, the opportunity to speak of the workload was a welcome one.

I asked each group about its experiences with welfare rights groups, and in a number of instances remained on with them as they continued their regular unit meetings. I made clear in the direct discussions that I was interested in understanding the full extent of responses to welfare rights demands and also that I was observing meetings in the agency and in the community to understand the usual pressures on staff.[9]

There were also many informal encounters and the phenomenon of what Dalton termed the "implicit analyst"—the person who can suggest leads to follow and who offers a sensitive evaluation as an insider.[10] I tried to balance the use of such staff to have varying points of view represented.

My efforts to observe welfare rights members in encounters with staff remained frustrated throughout. Such events happened at unpredictable times and the problem of getting to such encounters proved insurmountable, despite days of sitting in the waiting room and similar efforts. There were no agency documents or directives concerned with welfare rights organizations so that the recounted experiences of the staff constituted the primary sources of information about those interactions.

I extended my observations outward from the agency to include some appeal procedures at which recipients had welfare rights representation, public hearings of the state department of social welfare, the biweekly sessions of the welfare commission at which welfare rights groups were consistently in attendance. I also consulted the minutes of these meetings for the period before my study, which covered the lifetime of the groups in the city. I held interviews with some commissioners whose memberships spanned pre- and post-welfare-rights days, and observed meetings of the city's finance commission. The selection of community sources was determined by my interest in observing those situations in which welfare rights groups interacted with various levels of the welfare structure or with governmental bodies dealing with welfare issues.

Throughout this period of data collection, I made extensive field notes as soon after the event as possible. The analytic scheme delineated in the report was developed after I collected the data so that my recording was not limited or biased by preset categories.

But bias can enter in other ways. One of the potential sources of bias in any research is the reactive effects of the instrument; in the instance of an observational study, the researcher becomes an instrument. No doubt, a team of researchers in a setting such as this could offer greater safeguards against bias, but barring that, guidelines of reasonability and consistency can be employed. It seemed to me that at larger meetings my impact as an observer was minimal, at times nil, as was the case in public meetings. Within the agency, the staff members seemed so absorbed in the pressing problems of the workload that it seemed very unlikely that they could take the time and trouble to accommodate their behavior to my presence. In the smaller group meetings, and especially in direct discussions, there was more possibility of this. I attempted as far as possible to make my approach consistent within the different groups, and the range of viewpoints expressed seemed evidence of the lack of distorting effects. Also, there were times that groups of workers engaged in what seemed to be a continuation of discussions frequently held among themselves; at these times, they seemed unaware of my presence. I had purposely arranged to meet with staff members in their usual work groups in the hope that the presence of colleagues would act as a corrective mechanism for any tendency to report incidents or express viewpoints different from what they usually recounted to others.[11]

There may be other possibilities of distortion—the effects of my being a representative of academia,[12] of the self-selection of some informants,[13] of my selective observations or recording. A reasonable answer would lie in the internal consistency of the data. Thus, when I made certain observations at a divisional meeting, and later on, while sitting in on a unit meeting, I noted that a supervisor had reported agency events as discussed at that meeting in the same way, or when the same range of work pressures or responses to welfare rights interactions were reported in group after group, there would seem to be less concern about the observer as a biasing instrument.

The companion question is whether the final picture accurately represents the way things are. Is this description a valid reflection of agency pressures and welfare rights interaction? For the most part, a series of cross-checks helped to answer this question. In the area of agency pressures, for example, many other sources served to confirm staff members' statements about their workload: observations at administrative and unit meetings with many specific discussions of compliance with rules and work demands, observations in offices in which staff members attended to their own as well as uncovered caseloads, reading of manuals and directives, reports of delays in conversion plans because of workloads, statements in public meetings about application backlogs, and so on. Similarly with welfare rights encounters, the basic stance members assumed vis-à-vis the welfare system was amply illustrated in public meetings, in their own publications, in contacts with news media. The range of agency responses was corroborated as different staff members gave similar accounts.

After months of immersion in this kind of situation, the observer has a decided sense that the picture is as she reports it and feels frustrated in the ready ability to demonstrate this to others. As has been noted,

> the greater disadvantage in field work is the absence of methods for presenting its highly complex data and analytic procedure in abbreviated form so that readers can judge the plausibility of the researcher's inferences.[14]

ANALYSIS OF THE DATA

The study was begun with some general ideas about dilemmas for the welfare staff and pressures from welfare rights groups, but with an openness to explore their interaction and to evolve hypotheses. After the data were collected, the method developed by Glaser and Strauss—the constant comparative method —was used to analyze the data.[15]

Several examples of recorded observations and interviews were used to extract what appeared to be the basic elements of the process of interaction between the welfare system and welfare rights groups: the bind, the rules, the demands, and the responses. All of the data were then subject to a search for the properties of these elements by noting and comparing evidence in the different situations observed. Glaser and Strauss write:

> This constant comparison of the incidents very soon starts to generate theoretical properties of the category. One starts thinking in terms of the full range of types and continua of the category, its dimensions, the conditions under which it is pronounced or minimized, its major consequences, the relation of the category to other categories, and its other properties.[16]

This allowed for the full development of each of the four major factors of this interactional process and increased the likelihood of seeing their interdependence and evolving hypothetical statements about them. As the analysis continued, these basic categories were repeatedly considered to determine if their delineation and interconnections continued to make sense and reflect the process of interaction.

The intent has been to inquire into this area of social interaction in an exploratory manner, to describe the results of observations and interviews, and to suggest some hypotheses for further considerations and possible verification. Only additional studies can serve to confirm the usefulness of the ideas presented here about the process of interaction between clients and the public welfare system.

A FINAL NOTE

The report itself is offered in the belief that

> of course the exposition is more explicit and systematic, and the relevant implications more fully drawn out, but in the main outline, it can come as no surprise to leading officials.[17]

It is also offered in the conviction that social researchers, especially social workers, have both the right and the obligation to study the publicly accountable institutions that affect the welfare of people.

Notes

CHAPTER 1: INTRODUCTION

1. Peter M. Blau and W. Richard Scott, *Formal Organizations* (San Francisco: Chandler Publishing Co., 1962).

2. Alvin W. Gouldner, "Organizational Analysis," in *The Planning of Change*, eds. Warren G. Bennis, Kenneth D. Benne, Robert Chin (New York: Holt, Rinehart and Winston, 1961), pp. 393–99.

3. Carol Meyer, *Staff Development in Public Welfare Agencies* (New York: Columbia University Press, 1966); Gordon E. Brown, ed. *The Multi-Problem Dilemma* (Metuchen, New Jersey: The Scarecrow Press, Inc., 1968).

4. Joseph Gusfield, *Protest, Reform and Revolt* (New York: John Wiley and Sons, 1970).

5. John C. Donovan, *The Politics of Poverty* (New York: Pegasus, 1967); Ralph M. Kramer, *Participation of the Poor* (Englewood Cliffs, New Jersey: Prentice-Hall, 1969).

6. Richard A. Cloward and Richard M. Elman, "Poverty, Injustice and the Welfare State," *The Nation*, February 28, 1966, p. 234.

7. *Report of the National Advisory Commission on Civil Disorders* (New York: Dutton; paperback ed., Bantam Books, 1968).

CHAPTER 2: THE WELFARE SYSTEM BIND

1. *Having the Power, We Have the Duty*, Report on the Advisory Council on Public Welfare, June 1966; C. H. Meyer, *Staff Development in Public Welfare Agencies* (New York: Columbia University Press, 1966).

2. Gordon E. Brown, ed., *The Multi-Problem Dilemma* (Metuchen, New Jersey: The Scarecrow Press, Inc., 1968).

3. Eveline M. Burns, "What's Wrong with Public Welfare," *Social Service Review* 36 (June 1962): 111–22; Eveline M. Burns, "Future Social Security Policy and the APWA Leadership Role," *Public Welfare* 22 (Jan. 1964): 29–32; Richard A. Cloward and Frances Piven, "Politics, the Welfare System and Poverty, in *Poverty in America,* eds. Louis A. Ferman, Joyce L. Kornbluh, Alan Haber (Ann Arbor: University of Michigan Press, 1965) pp. 223–39; Edward A. Sparer, "The Role of the Welfare Client's Lawyer," *UCLA Law Review* 12 (1965): 361–80.

4. Mencher suggests that the Medieval Church's indiscriminate almsgiving was a threat to later society's stress on work, making it necessary for programs to exercise control over the recipient's motivation to work and to change him as well as aid him. Samuel Mencher, "The Changing Balance of Status and Contract in Assistance Policy," *Social Service Review* 35 (1961): 17–32.

5. Theodore Sarbin, "Poverty and Social Identity," Paper presented at Conference on Psychological Factors in Poverty, University of Wisconsin, June 1967.

6. Daniel R. Mandelker, "Judicial Review in General Assistance," *Journal of Public Law* 6 (1957): 100.

7. George Simmel, "The Poor," *Social Problems* 13 (1965): 136.

8. This statement was made to me in a research interview, part of a study of new recipients. The study has been reported in Scott Briar, "Welfare from Below," in *Law of the Poor,* ed. Jacobus ten Broek (San Francisco: Chandler Publishing Co., 1966).

9. A Loudoun County, Virginia, tenant farmer on the CBS telecast "Hunger in America," May 21, 1968.

10. Alvin S. Gouldner, "The Norm of Reciprocity: A Preliminary Statement," *American Sociological Review* 25 (1960): 161–78.

11. *Ibid.,* p. 171.

12. Marcel Mauss, *The Gift* (New York: W. W. Norton and Co., 1967), p. 58.

13. Meg Greenfield, "The 'Welfare Chiselers' of Newburgh, N.Y.," *The Reporter,* Aug. 17, 1961, p. 39.

14. Simmel, "The Poor," p. 122.

15. Robert Conot, *Rivers of Blood: Years of Darkness* (New York: Bantam Books, 1968), p. 436. (The hardcover edition was published by William Morrow.)

16. Bernard Beck, "Welfare as a Moral Category," *Social Problems* 14 (Winter 1967): 260, 261, 264.

17. In his critique of the Moynihan report Jencks agrees with Beck's thesis: "Moynihan's analysis is in the conservative tradition that guided

the drafting of the poverty program (in whose formulation he partici-
pated . . .). The guiding assumption is that social pathology is caused less
by basic defects in the social system than by defects in particular individuals and groups which prevent their adjusting to the system. The prescription is therefore to change the deviants, not the system." Christopher
Jencks, "The Moynihan Report" in *The Moynihan Report and the
Politics of Controversy*, eds. Lee Rainwater and William L. Yancey (Cambridge, Mass.: MIT Press, 1967), p. 443.

18. Senate Committee on Finance; Hearings on H.R. 12080, September
1967.

19. Gary Allen, "War on Poverty," *American Opinion*, February 1968,
p. 22.

20. "Hunger in America," CBS Telecast, May 21, 1968.

21. Phillipe Nonet, *Administrative Justice* (New York: Russell Sage
Foundation, 1969), p. 91.

22. These data are for October 1972. *Public Assistance Statistics, October, 1972*, U.S. Department of Health, Education and Welfare, Feb. 9,
1973.

23. Nathan Glazer, "A Sociologist's View of Poverty," in *Poverty in
America*, ed. Margaret S. Gordon (San Francisco: Chandler Publishing
Co., 1965), p. 16.

24. Burns (among others) makes the unorthodox suggestion that we
might find that some families would not be "problems" or need services if
their monthly grants were adequate. Burns, "Future Social Security Policy" (1964), p. 31.

25. Gilbert Y. Steiner, *Social Insecurity* (Chicago: Rand McNally & Co.,
1966), pp. 176 ff.

26. For discussion of the "lower class culture" view, see, for example,
Oscar Lewis, "The Culture of Poverty," *Scientific American* 215 (1966):
19–25; Walter B. Miller, "Lower Class Culture as a Generating Milieu of
Gang Delinquency," *Journal of Social Issues* 14 (1958): 5–20; For ques-
tioning of this position, see, for example, S. M. Miller, Frank Riessman,
Arthur Seagull, "Poverty and Self-Indulgence: A Critique of the Non-
Deferred Gratification Pattern," in Ferman, *Poverty in America;* Alvin
Schorr, "The Nonculture of Poverty," *American Journal of Orthopsychia-
try* 34 (1964): 907–12; Suzanne Keller and Marisa Zavalloni, "Ambition
and Social Class," *Social Forces* 43 (1964): 58–70.

27. Brown, *Multi-Problem Dilemma;* Dorothy Miller *et al.*, "Effectiveness of Social Services to AFDC Families," in *California Welfare*, Assembly Committee on Social Welfare, 1969, Appendix I; Reed V. Clegg, *The
Administrator in Public Welfare* (Springfield, Illinois: Charles C.
Thomas, 1966), p. 122.

28. Even without proof of results, Congress had an interesting predilec-

tion for allocating increasingly more money for services. Davis McEntire and Joanne Haworth, "The Two Functions of Public Welfare: Income Maintenance and Social Services," *Social Work* 12 (1967): 122.

29. John Kenneth Galbraith, *The Affluent Society* (Boston: Houghton Mifflin, 1958).

30. See, for example, James C. Vadakin, *Children, Poverty and Family Allowances* (New York: Basic Books, 1968); Robert Lampman, "End and Means in War on Poverty" in *Poverty Amid Affluence,* ed. Leo Fishman (New Haven: Yale University Press, 1966); Eveline Burns, "Childhood Poverty and the Children's Allowance", in *Children's Allowances and the Economic Welfare of Children* (New York: Citizens Committee for Children, 1968). Christopher Green, "The Negative Income Tax" in Ferman, *Poverty in America.*

31. Ten Broek, *Law of the Poor.*

32. Joel F. Handler, "Controlling Official Behavior in Welfare Administration" in ten Broek, *Law of the Poor.*

33. *Ibid.*

34. Sparer, "Welfare Client's Lawyer," p. 369.

35. Charles Reich, "Individual Rights and Social Welfare: The Emerging Legal Issues," *Yale Law Journal* 74 (1965): 1247.

36. Jerome Carlin and Jan Howard, "Legal Representation and Class Justice," *UCLA Law Review* 12 (1965): 425.

37. Charles Reich, "Midnight Welfare Searches and the Social Security Act," *Yale Law Journal* 72 (1963): 1355.

38. Edwin E. Witte, *The Development of the Social Security Act* (Madison: University of Wisconsin Press, 1962), p. 163; See also Wilbur Cohen, "Factors Influencing the Content of Federal Public Welfare Legislation," *The Social Welfare Forum* (National Conference of Social Welfare, 1954).

39. Steiner, *Social Insecurity,* p. 23.

40. Daniel Moynihan, "The Crises in Welfare," *The Public Interest* 10 (1968): 5.

41. John A. Hamilton, "Will 'Work' Work?" *Saturday Review,* May 23, 1970, p. 25.

42. For data on overrepresentation of nonwhites in the AFDC population see Lora S. Collins, "Public Assistance Expenditures in the United States," in *Studies in the Economics of Income Maintenance,* ed. Otto Eckstein (Washington, D.C.: Brookings Institute, 1967).

43. Greenleigh Associates, *Facts, Fallacies and the Future* (New York: Greenleigh Associates, 1960); Henry Miller, "Characteristics of AFDC Families," *Social Service Review* 34 (1965): 399–409.

44. Steiner, *Social Insecurity,* p. 116.

45. J. M. Wedemeyer and Percy Moore, "The American Welfare System" in ten Broek, *Law of the Poor,* p. 27.

46. "Social caseworkers know from several decades of sad experience

that legal compulsion is rarely successful in obtaining compliance from these fathers." Harold L. Wilensky and Charles N. Lebeaux, *Industrial Society and Social Welfare* (New York: The Free Press, 1965), p. 179. See also Clegg, *Administrator in Public Welfare,* pp. 130 ff. on the "elusive search for the absent father."

47. Steiner makes the point that the restrictions instituted at Newburgh, New York, in 1961 and which created such a furor are just an exaggeration of others in force elsewhere. Newburgh imposed these restrictions all at once; others do it one or two at a time. Steiner, *Social Insecurity,* pp. 108 ff.

48. Walter Gellhorn, *When Americans Complain* (Cambridge, Mass.: Harvard University Press, 1966), p. 196.

49. Compare Goffman's similar method for characterizing the total institution. Erving Goffman, *Asylums* (New York: Doubleday, Anchor Books, 1961).

50. On repeated occasions when the subject of welfare rights organizations has arisen in private conversations with persons unfamiliar professionally with public welfare, they have been uniformly surprised, almost aghast, that recipients should be anything but grateful for their aid, and do anything but try to get off welfare as soon as possible.

51. References to professionalism among public welfare staff members are made with awareness that only a minority of workers and supervisors have complete graduate training. See the discussion in chapter 6 about the role of professionalism here, notwithstanding the proportion of trained staff.

52. Charles F. Grosser and Edward Sparer, "Social Welfare and Social Justice," in *Community Action Against Poverty,* by George Brager and Francis Purcell (New Haven: College and University Press, 1967).

53. Blau and Scott recognize the conflict of interest for the professional social worker, who must also determine eligibility; but such conflict is not given the emphasis it receives here. Peter M. Blau and W. Richard Scott, *Formal Organizations* (San Francisco: Chandler Publishing Co., 1962), p. 190. See also Harry A. Wasserman, "The Moral Posture of the Social Worker in a Public Agency," *Public Welfare* 25 (1967): 38–44.

54. Donald R. Cressey, "Achievement of an Unstated Organizational Goal," in *Complex Organizations,* ed. Amitai Etzioni (New York: Holt, Rinehart and Winston, 1965).

55. The concept of the bind was not part of the initial guiding questions for the study. Rather it evolved from discussion with staff (and observations) about their work pressures and experiences with welfare rights members.

56. See, for example, Meyer, *Staff Development;* Edwin Thomas and Donna McLeod, *In-Service Training and Reduced Caseloads* (New York: Russell Sage Foundation, 1960).

57. At the time of the study, all but a handful of the more than 40 AFDC units had missing workers and, as someone remarked, even those were "wobbly."

58. An intake worker reported an experiment he embarked on to try to establish (wholly within regulations) the eligibility of every applicant. He found that it was possible to do so for most applicants—many of whom would have been denied aid normally—but he estimated it took him ten times as long.

59. For discussions of factors of this nature, see, for example, W. Richard Scott, "Professional Employees in a Bureaucratic Structure," in *The Semi-Professions and Their Organization*, ed. Amitai Etzioni (New York: Free Press, 1969; Andrew Billingsley, "The Role of the Social Worker in a Child Protective Agency," *Child Welfare* 43 (1964): 472–79.

60. W. Richard Scott, "A Case Study of Professional Workers in a Bureaucratic Setting," Ph.D. dissertation, University of Chicago, 1961.

61. See Gell's fictionalized account of such attitudes in public welfare. Frank Gell, *The Black Badge* (New York: Harper and Row, 1969).

62. See chapter 6 for discussion of professionalism in a fuller sense.

63. Nonet describes the early "welfare approach" of the Industrial Accident Commission in California when demands of employees were not to be taken at face value but were rather seen as manifestations of "real, underlying problems" which the agency, not the worker, was to define. Nonet, *Administrative Justice*, p. 256.

64. Miller and Rein claim that because of the mistaken notion that casework will help the welfare recipient, workers have forsaken humane principles that would acknowledge the need for money, for aid as a right, and for freedom to choose services. S. M. Miller and Martin Rein, "Will the War on Poverty Change America?" *Transaction* 2 (1965): 17–22.

65. Peter Blau, *The Dynamics of Bureaucracy* (Chicago: University of Chicago Press, 1955); Phillip Marcus, "Expressive and Instrumental Groups: Toward a Theory of Group Structure," *American Journal of Sociology* 66 (1960): 54–59.

66. The evidence here was similar to other experiences in the helping professions when humor that seems almost grotesque relieves tensions about very serious client situations. See Blau and Scott, *Formal Organizations*.

CHAPTER 3: WELFARE RULES

1. Philip Selznick, "Foundations of the Theory of Organization," *American Sociological Review* 13 (1948): 25–35.

2. Alan Keith-Lucas, *Decisions About People in Need* (Chapel Hill: University of North Carolina Press, 1957), p. 210.

3. Gouldner writes of the place of continual supervision in this super-structure of control and suggests the supervision takes place because of the awareness that workers really can't believe in the philosophy of the agency. Alvin Gouldner, "The Secrets of Organizations," *The Social Welfare Forum* (National Conference of Social Welfare, 1963).

4. Harold L. Wilensky and Charles N. Lebeaux, *Industrial Society in Social Welfare* (New York: The Free Press, 1965), p. 240.

5. Gideon Sjoberg, Richard Brymer, and Buford Farris, "Bureaucracy and the Lower Class," *Sociology and Sociological Research* 50 (1966): 325.

6. W. Richard Scott, "Professional Employees in a Bureaucratic Structure," in *The Semi-Professions and Their Organization*, ed. Amitai Etzioni (New York: Free Press, 1969); Edwin Thomas and Donna McLeod, *In-Service Training and Reduced Caseloads* (New York: Russell Sage Foundation, 1960.).

7. Sjoberg, et al., "Bureaucracy." Cohen found among employment agency staff whose tensions might be considered not quite so severe as welfare workers an "intolerable human strain of client requests for rule breaking, on the one hand and on the other hand, the stream of formal rules and procedures." Harry Cohen, *The Demonics of Bureaucracy* (Ames, Iowa: Iowa State University Press, 1965), p. 226.

8. Robert K. Merton, "Bureaucratic Structure and Personality," in Etzioni, *Semi-Professions*.

9. *Having the Power, We Have the Duty*, Report on the Advisory Council on Public Welfare, June 1966. Burns counters that public assistance budgeting is "inherently destructive of an individual's self-esteem and privacy." Eveline M. Burns, "Future Social Security Policy and the APWA Leadership Role," *Public Welfare* 22 (Jan. 1964): 29.

10. Thomas and McLeod, *In-Service Training*, p. 96. Emphasis added.

11. Scott, in Etzioni, *Semi-Professions*, p. 119.

12. Everett C. Hughes, *Men and Their Work* (Glencoe, Illinois: Free Press, 1958), p. 49.

13. Alvin Gouldner, "Red Tape as a Social Problem," in Robert Merton, et al., *Reader in Bureaucracy* (Glencoe, Illinois: Free Press, 1963).

14. Commenting on the requirement that workers be held responsible for any errors in the extensive eligibility investigation, Hoshino asks, "Who is being checked on—the worker or the client?" George Hoshino, "Program, Policies and the Task of the Public Welfare Worker," *Public Welfare* 26 (1968): 127.

15. Wilensky and Lebeaux, *Industrial Society*, p. 246.

16. Reed V. Clegg, *The Administrator in Public Welfare* (Springfield, Illinois: Charles C. Thomas, 1966), p. 27. There was a partly humorous illustration of the degree that regulations are adhered to. A recipient had some earned income during one month, which reduced the grant for which she was eligible to $2.00. Because regulations prescribe that an

AFDC grant is to be paid in two equal parts, she received $1.00 on the first of the month and $1.00 on the sixteenth.

17. *Ibid.*, p. 27.

18. Richard A. Cloward and Richard M. Elman, "Poverty Injustice and the Welfare State, Part II," *The Nation*, March 7, 1966, p. 265.

19. Edward A. Sparer, "The Role of the Welfare Client's Lawyer," *UCLA Law Review* 12 (1965): 373.

20. Charles Reich, "Individual Rights and Social Welfare: The Emerging Legal Issues," *Yale Law Journal* 74 (1965): 1252.

21. See Cohen, and Francis and Stone, for similar behavior in other public bureaucracies and instances of upper-level decisions being thereby based on incorrect information. Wilbur Cohen, "Factors Influencing the Content of Federal Public Welfare Legislation," in *The Social Welfare Forum* (National Conference of Social Welfare, 1954); Roy G. Francis and Robert Stone, *Service and Procedure in Bureaucracy* (Minneapolis: University of Minnesota, 1956).

22. *Operation Big City,* Report of the United States Department of Health, Education and Welfare, October 1965.

23. Charles Reich, "Midnight Welfare Searches and the Social Security Act," *Yale Law Journal* 72 (1963): 1347–1360. Scott Briar, "Welfare from Below," in *Law of the Poor,* ed. Jacobus ten Broek (San Francisco: Chandler Publishing Co., 1966).

CHAPTER 4: THE RECIPIENT DEMANDS

1. Edgar S. Cahn, "Discussion" (of paper by Riessman) in *Poverty in America,* ed. Margaret S. Gordon (San Francisco: Chandler Publishing Co., 1965), p. 427.

2. Nonet's description of the changed relationship between the Industrial Accident Commission and disabled workers may be even more to the point, since in its early period the Commission viewed the workers from a "welfare" perspective. Only as the legal rights of workers were expanded, to a great extent thanks to the support of the developing labor movement, did that perspective begin to change. Phillipe Nonet, *Administrative Justice* (New York: Russell Sage Foundation, 1969).

3. Richard Cloward and Richard Elman, "Advocacy in the Ghetto," *Transaction* 4 (1966): 27–35; Richard Cloward and Frances Piven, "We've Got Rights: The No-Longer Silent Welfare Poor," *The New Republic* 158 (Aug. 5, 1967): 23–24.

4. Joseph E. Paull, "Recipients Aroused: The New Welfare Rights Movement," *Social Work* 12 (1967): 101.

5. Personal communication from Dr. George Wiley, Executive Director, National Welfare Rights Organization.

6. In 1969, the United States Department of Labor entered into a contract with the National Welfare Rights Organization regarding the Work Incentive Program. *Christian Science Monitor,* Nov. 18, 1969.

7. Paull, "Recipients Aroused," p. 106.

8. Warren C. Haggstrom, "Can the Poor Transform the World?" in *Among the People,* eds. Irwin Deutscher and Elizabeth Thompson (New York: Basic Books, 1968), p. 96.

9. A poverty lawyer stated that although legal services give welfare rights members much support, this is not a one-way street. Welfare rights activity is often needed to police the legal rulings that legal services have been instrumental in changing; furthermore, only by massive recipient pressure does he believe that meaningful changes can take place in the welfare system.

10. During that period, I happened to be in an anteroom reading case records for another research project, while a conference of administrators was considering, in panicky tones, what to do about a welfare rights group that had set up an informational table outside the building. At the time, the staff's reaction seemed far out of proportion to the supposed threat. In view of what the staff members described during this study, they may very well have expected far more than just an informational table.

11. Haggstrom states that this "early militancy was regarded as inexplicable ingratitude, demonstrating incredible naivete and probably provoked by outside agitators." Haggstrom, in Deutscher and Thompson, *Among the People,* p. 85.

12. As a point of contrast, Clark notes an institution—the adult education program—that must be extremely sensitive to its clientele, as it is wholly dependent on their continued attendance if the program is to continue. Burton R. Clark, "Organizational Adaptation and Precarious Values," in *Complex Organizations,* ed. Amitai Etzioni (New York: Holt, Rinehart and Winston, 1965).

13. George Brager and Harry Specht, "Mobilizing the Poor for Social Action," *Social Welfare Forum* (National Conference on Social Welfare, 1965), p. 201.

14. Coser discusses the way in which social conflict (as distinct from personal and diffuse hostility) "necessarily changes the previous terms of the relationship of the participants." Lewis Coser, *Functions of Social Conflict* (New York: The Free Press, 1956), p. 40.

15. Walter Gellhorn, *When Americans Complain* (Cambridge, Mass.: Harvard University Press, 1966), p. 197.

16. Becker notes a similar phenomenon within the "authority system of the public school." Teachers fear that the intrusion of parents, even on legitimate grounds, will lead to illegitimate parental control. The parent appears as an unpredictable, uncontrollable agent. Howard S. Becker,

"The Teacher in the Authority System of the Public School," in Etzioni, *Complex Organizations.*

17. Handler observes that there are in fact insufficient controls over workers in terms of arbitrary actions—see the elasticity of rules discussed earlier—and that the complaining client constitutes one such needed method of control. Joel Handler, "Report on Research in Progress," presented at Center for Study of Law and Society, University of California, Berkeley, Spring 1970. Also, in Blau and Scott's discussion of the service organization, they note that the "failure to serve the welfare of clients is probably a more prevalent problem than becoming subservient to them" —a further conformation of the need for the pro-client control Handler urges. Peter M. Blau and W. Richard Scott, *Formal Organizations* (San Francisco: Chandler Publishing Co., 1962), p. 53.

CHAPTER 5: THE AGENCY RESPONSES

1. Philip Selznick, "Foundations of the Theory of Organization," *American Sociological Review* 13 (1948): 25–35.

2. *Ibid.;* Lewis Coser, *Continuities in the Study of Social Conflict* (New York: The Free Press, 1967), p. 23.

3. Peter Blau, *The Dynamics of Bureaucracy* (Chicago: University of Chicago Press, 1955), p. 263.

4. Howard S. Becker, "The Teacher in the Authority System of the Public School," in *Complex Organizations,* ed. Amitai Etzioni (New York: Holt, Rinehart and Winston, 1965).

5. Robert Habenstein and Edwin Christ, *Professionalizer, Traditionalizer, and Utilizer* (Columbia, Missouri: University of Missouri Press, 1955).

6. Seymour M. Lipset, "Bureaucracy and Social Reform" in Etzioni, *Complex Organizations,* p. 265.

7. Gideon Sjoberg, Richard Brymer, and Buford Farris, "Bureaucracy and the Lower Class," *Sociology and Sociological Research* 50 (1966): 325.

8. Richard A. Cloward and Frances Piven, "Politics, the Welfare System and Poverty," in *Poverty in America,* eds. Louis A. Ferman, Joyce L. Kornbluh, Alan Haber (Ann Arbor: University of Michigan Press, 1965), p. 232.

9. Robert Pruger and Harry Specht, "Establishing New Careers Program: Organizational Barriers and Strategies," *Social Work* 13 (1968): 25. Termed "mutual invisibility" here, a like phenomenon is evident in the study cited earlier in which client and social worker formulation of the client's problem were at opposite poles. S. M. Miller, Frank

Riessman, Arthur Seagull, "Poverty and Self-Indulgence: A Critique of the Non-Deferred Gratification Pattern," in Ferman, et al. *Poverty in America.*

10. George Brager and Harry Specht, "Mobilizing the Poor for Social Action," *Social Welfare Forum* (National Conference on Social Welfare, 1965), p. 202.

11. Sparer disparages the notion of the "good guy" theory of government and supports a system of legal rights for recipients, among other reasons, because of the political constraints on the administrator. Edward Sparer, "The New Public Law," in George Brager and Francis Purcell, *Community Action Against Poverty* (New Haven: College and University Press, 1967), p. 308.

12. Glazer notes the difference between the more adaptable welfare institution in Europe and the American institution unresponsive to the needs of low-income people. Nathan Glazer, "A Sociologist's View of Poverty," in *Poverty in America,* ed. Margaret S. Gordon (San Francisco: Chandler Publishing Co., 1965), p. 23.

13. Blau, *Dynamics of Bureaucracy,* p. 263.

14. See Lipsky for an analysis of tactics developed in response to tenants' strikes, which in some respects parallel the responses to be described here. Michael Lipsky, "Protest as a Political Resource," *American Political Science Review* 62 (1968): 1144–1158.

15. Erving Goffman, "On Cooling the Mark Out: Some Aspects of Adaptation to Failure," in *Human Behavior and Social Processes,* ed. Arnold Rose (Boston: Houghton Mifflin Company, 1962).

16. George Brager and Harry Specht, "Social Action by the Poor" in Brager and Purcell, *Community Action Against Poverty,* p. 140.

17. Charles F. Grosser and Edward Sparer, "Social Welfare and Social Justice," in Brager and Purcell, *Community Action Against Poverty,* p. 298.

18. Philip Selznick, *TVA and the Grass Roots* (New York: Harper and Row, 1966), p.35.

19. *Ibid.,* p.13.

20. *Ibid.,* p. 64.

21. *Ibid.,* p. 259.

22. *Ibid.,* p. 217.

23. The application of co-optation to a public housing situation may be closer to the welfare example than Selznick's TVA. In this, citizen participation was described as a co-optation device which progressively committed the citizens to the plan while their right to dissent was being undercut. Peter H. Rossi, "Theory, Research and Practice in Community Organization," in *Social Science and Community Action,* ed. Charles Adrian (East Lansing, Michigan: Michigan State University Press, 1960).

24. See Coser's discussion of increasing expectations of a social contribution of the poor as a way out of poverty. Lewis A. Coser, "The Sociology of Poverty," *Social Problems* 13 (1965): 141–148.

25. The recent Supreme Court ruling that the right to a hearing before aid is discontinued is a landmark because it establishes aid as a property right, subject to the same legal protections as other property rights. Goldberg v. Kelly, 38 U.S.L.W. 4223 (U. S., March 23, 1970).

26. Frank Riessman, "Anti-Poverty Programs and the Role of the Poor," in *Poverty in America,* ed. Margaret S. Gordon (San Francisco: Chandler Publishing Co., 1965), p. 412.

27. A legal services attorney wondered, in conversation, about the long-range results of welfare rights and legal pressures in view of the impressive capacity of the welfare system to initiate countermeasures with possible worse consequences for recipients than the original problem.

28. Carol Ruth Silver, "How to Handle a Welfare Case," *Law in Transition Quarterly* 4 (1967): 100.

29. J. M. Wedemeyer and Percy Moore, "The American Welfare System," in *Law of the poor,* ed. Jacobus ten Broek (San Francisco: Chandler Publishing Co., 1966), p. 18.

CHAPTER 6: CATALYSTS FOR CHANGE

1. These considerations are meant to apply to professions in other organizational settings, though here they are addressed primarily to the staff of the public welfare system as possible initiators of change within that system. However see discussions on pp. 104 ff. concerning the ambiguities of professionalism in public welfare, as well as realistic limitations on staff potential to effect change. Chapter 8 deals specifically with the question of applicability of these welfare-focused discussions to other institutions.

2. Eliot Freidson, *The Profession of Medicine* (New York: Dodd, Mead and Co., 1970), p. 82.

3. Ernest Greenwood, "Attributes of a Profession," *Social Work* 2 (1957): 46.

4. Freidson, *Profession of Medicine*, p. 83.

5. Greenwood, *Attributes of a Profession,* p. 50.

6. Greenwood, for example, includes, in addition to a theory base and professional authority, the requirement of community sanction, a regulative code of ethics, and a professional culture. *Ibid.*

7. Sidney Bernard and Philip Booth, "The Public Assistance Power Structure," in *Can Public Welfare Keep Pace?,* ed. Malvin Morton (New York: Columbia University Press, 1969), p. 16.

8. James R. Dumpson, "Public Welfare: Recommitted, Restructured, Revitalized" in Morton, *Public Welfare*, pp. 48–49.

9. Peter Blau and Richard Scott, *Formal Organizations* (San Francisco: Chandler Publishing Co., 1962), p. 53. See also recent discussions of challenges to the monopoly of professionals in the control of service: Freidson, *Profession of Medicine;* Marie Huag and Marvin Sussman, "Professional Autonomy and the Revolt of the Client," *Social Problems* 17 (1969): 153–60.

10. Dumpson, in Morton, *Public Welfare*, p. 48.

11. Davis McEntire and Joanne Haworth, "The Two Functions of Public Welfare: Income Maintenance and Social Services," *Social Work* 12 (1967): 23–31.

12. Kermit Wiltse, "Social Casework Services in the Aid to Dependent Children Program" *Social Service Review* 28 (1954): 173–85.

13. Dorothy Miller, et al., "Effectiveness of Social Services to AFDC Families," in *California Welfare*, Appendix I, Assembly Committee on Social Welfare, 1969.

14. Gordon Brown, *The Multi-Problem Dilemma* (Metuchen, New Jersey: The Scarecrow Press, 1968). See discussions there of the restrictive influence of public assistance settings on casework efforts. Also see earlier reference to the comment in Pruger and Specht on the wide disparity between the overriding concerns of the social worker and those of the client. Robert Pruger and Harry Specht, "Establishing New Career Programs: Organizational Barriers and Strategies" *Social Work* 13 (1968), pp. 21–32.

15. Herb Bisno, "How Social Will Social Work Be?" *Social Work* 1 (1956): 12–18; Greenwood, *Attributes of a Profession.*

16. Irwin Epstein, "Social Workers and Social Action: Attitudes toward Social Action Strategies," *Social Work* 13 (1968): 101–108; W. Joseph Heffernan, Jr. "Political Activity and Social Work Executives," *Social Work* 9 (1964): 18–23.

17. Daniel Thursz, "Social Action as a Professional Responsibility," *Social Work* 11 (1966): 12–21; Hyman Wiener, "Social Change and Social Group Work Practice" *Social Work* 9 (1964): 106–112.

18. See, for example, W. Richard Scott, "A Case Study of Professional Workers in a Bureaucratic Setting" (Ph.D. Dissertation, University of Chicago, 1961): Andrew Billingsley, "Bureaucratic and Professional Orientation Patterns in Social Casework," *Social Service Review* 38 (1954): 400–407.

19. For a fuller explanation of a challenge to this position, see Brown, *Multi-Problem Dilemma*. For the same argument in a somewhat different setting, see Ludwig Geismar and Jane Krisberg, *The Forgotten Neighborhood* (Metuchen, New Jersey: The Scarecrow Press, 1967).

20. See Frances Fox Piven and Richard A. Cloward, *Regulating the*

Poor (New York: Pantheon, 1971) for a recent perspective on this issue. The authors claim that welfare programs "are intended to control social unrest and to enforce work at low wages." See also Alvin L. Schorr "Why Enforced Work Won't Work in Welfare," *Saturday Review*, June 19, 1971, p. 19.

21. Robert K. Merton, *Social Theory and Social Structure* (New York: The Free Press, 1968), p. 273.

22. George Brager, "Institutional Change: Perimeters of the Possible," *Social Work* 12 (1967): 64.

23. Ruth Pauley, "The Public Welfare Agency of the Future" *Social Casework* 47 (1966): 288.

24. Charles Grosser, "Community Development Programs Serving the Urban Poor," *Social Work* 10 (1965): 16.

25. Robert Sunley, "Family Advocacy: From Case to Cause," *Social Casework* 51 (1970): 350.

26. Martin Rein, "Social Work in Search of a Radical Profession," *Social Work* 13 (1970): 17.

27. A. D. Green, "The Professional Worker in a Bureaucracy," *Social Service Review* 40 (1966): 74.

28. For discussion of a current educational plan to meet these contradictions in training, see Rino Patti and Herman Resnick, "Education for Social Change," *Social Work Education Reporter* 20 (1972): 62–66; Rino Patti and Herman Resnick, "Changing the Agency from Within," *Social Work* 17 (1972): 48–57.

29. Rein, "Radical Profession."

30. Phillipe Nonet, *Administrative Justice* (New York: The Russell Sage Foundation, 1969).

31. Compare Piven and Cloward, *Regulating the Poor.*

32. In an historical review of social work that yet has contemporary significance, Becker writes that "the profession attempted to mediate between the needs of the poor, *as the social worker, not the poor, defined them,* and the rights of the rest of society," Dorothy Becker, "Social Welfare Leaders as Spokesmen for the Poor," *Social Casework* 44 (1968): 89. Emphasis added.

33. Nonet, *Administrative Justice,* p. 93.

34. Rein, "Radical Profession," p. 27.

35. John B. Turner, "In Response to Change: Social Work at the Crossroads" *Social Work* 13 (1968): 14.

36. This kind of orientation, found here to be a deviation both from the bureaucratic and the professional adaptations to the bind, has received little attention. For exceptions, see Irving Kermish and Frank Kushin, "Why High Turnover: Social Work Staff Losses in a County Welfare Department," *Public Welfare* 27 (1960): 134–39; John L. Ehrlich,

"Breaking the Dole Barrier: The Lingering Death of an American Welfare System," *Social Work* 14 (1969): 49–57.

37. David Mechanic, "Sources of Power of Lower Participants in Complex Organizations," *Administrative Science Quarterly* 7 (1962): 355.

38. Alvin Gouldner, "The Secrets of Organizations," *Social Welfare Forum*, 1963, pp. 161–77.

39. John Ehrlich and John Tropman, "The Politics of Participation: Student Power," *Social Work* 14 (1969): 65.

40. Almost as a by-product, these workers may also undermine or at least ignore the social work profession's assignment of low prestige to them. See Blau and Scott, *Formal Organizations,* and Clark's discussion of "not fully legitimized functionaries" for accounts of this lowered prestige. Burton Clark, "Organizational Adaptation and Precarious Values," in *Complex Organizations,* ed. Amitai Etzioni (New York: Holt, Rinehart and Winston, 1965), pp. 159–67.

41. David Vail, *Dehumanization and the Institutional Career* (Springfield, Illinois: Charles C. Thomas, 1966), pp. 44, 51.

42. Erving Goffman, *Asylums* (Chicago: Aldine Publishing Company, 1961), p. 5.

43. *Ibid.,* p. 24.

44. *Ibid.,* p. 84.

45. Scott Briar, "Welfare from Below," in Jacobus ten Broek, ed., *Law of the Poor* (San Francisco: Chandler Publishing Company, 1966).

46. Goffman, *Asylums,* p. 23.

47. *Ibid.,* p. 43.

48. Dumpson, in Morton, *Public Welfare,* p. 66.

49. Goffman, *Asylums,* p. 37.

50. *Ibid.,* p. 48.

51. Chris Argyris, *Integrating the Individual and the Organization* (New York: John Wiley and Sons, 1964), p. 293.

52. Viola W. Bernard, Perry Ottenberg, and Fritz Redl, "Dehumanization: A Composite Psychological Defense in Relation to Modern War," in *The Triple Revolution,* eds. Robert Perrucci and Marc Pilisuk (Boston: Little, Brown and Company, 1938), pp. 19–20.

53. *Ibid.,* pp. 25–28.

54. Vail, *Dehumanization,* p. 68.

55. Green, for example, believes that the worker loses effectiveness if he overidentifies with his client in this regard. Green, "Professional Worker."

56. Scott Briar, "The Social Worker's Responsibility for the Civil Rights of Clients," *New Perspectives* 1 (1967): 91.

57. David Wineman and Adrienne James, "The Advocacy Challenge to Schools of Social Work," *Social Work* 14 (1969): 23.

58. Freidson, *Profession of Medicine*, p. 377.

59. Viola Bernard, et al., in Perrucci and Pilisuk, *Triple Revolution*, p. 30.

60. Michael Lipsky, "Protest as a Political Resource," *American Political Science Review* 62 (1968): 1145.

61. Dumpson, in Morton, *Public Welfare*, p. 64.

CHAPTER 7: CHANGE STRATEGIES

1. For the argument concerning the central importance of the state administrator on local welfare programs, see Sidney Bernard and Philip Booth, "The Public Assistance Power Structure," in *Can Public Welfare Keep Pace?*, ed. Malvin Morton (New York: Columbia University Press, 1969).

2. See, for example, Daniel Katz and Robert L. Kahn, *The Social Psychology of Organizations* (New York: John Wiley and Sons, 1966); Elliott Jaques, *The Changing Culture of a Factory* (London: Tavistock Publications, Ltd., 1951).

3. Warren Bennis, "Beyond Bureaucracy," *Transaction* 2 (1965): 31–35.

4. Chris Argyris, *Integrating the Individual and the Organization* (New York: John Wiley and Sons, 1964), p. 168.

5. David Mechanic, "Sources of Power of Lower Participants in Complex Organizations," *Administrative Science Quarterly* 7 (1962): 349–64.

6. Donald R. Cressey, "Contradictory Directives in Complex Organization: The Case of the Prison," *Administrative Science Quarterly* 4 (1959): 19.

7. George Brager, "Institutional Change: Perimeters of the Possible," *Social Work* 12 (1967): 65.

8. Jacques, *Changing Culture*, p. 306.

9. Jan Howard and Robert Somers, "Resisting Institutional Evil from Within," paper read at Conference on the Legitimation of Evil, San Francisco, February 1970.

10. Regarding shifts of roles, see David R. Hunter, "Social Action to Influence Institutional Change," *Social Casework* 5 (1970): 225–31.

11. Victor A. Thompson, "Bureaucracy and Innovation," *Administrative Science Quarterly* 10 (1965): 11.

12. Argyris, *Integrating the Individual*, p. 59.

13. James D. Thompson and William J. McEwen, "Organizational Goals and Environment: Goal Setting as an Interactional Process," in *Social Welfare Institutions*, ed. Mayer N. Zald (New York: John Wiley and Sons, 1965), p. 414.

14. For a description of an innovative educational plan to develop skills in social work students for the implementation of system changes,

see Rino Patti and Herman Resnick, "Education for Social Change," *Social Work Education Reporter* 20 (1972): 62–66; Rino Patti and Herman Resnick, "Changing the Agency from Within," *Social Work* 17 (1972): 48–57.

15. Briar's study of fair hearing procedures in California indicated that *any* outside representation at the hearing significantly increased the recipient's chances for a favorable decision. Scott Briar, "The Current Crisis in Casework," in *Social Work Practice*, 1967 (New York: Columbia University Press, 1967), p. 29.

16. James Dumpson, "Public Welfare: Recommitted, Restructured, Revitalized," in *Can Public Welfare Keep Pace?*, ed. Malvin Morton (New York: Columbia University Press, 1969), p. 70.

17. Hyman Wiener, "Social Change and Social Group Work Practice," *Social Work* 9 (1964): 106–112. Studies such as those by Epstein and Heffernan also imply that the social action social workers might approve of or engage in would be separate from their work roles. Irwin Epstein, "Social Workers and Social Action: Attitudes toward Social Action Strategies," *Social Work* 13 (1968): 101–108; W. Joseph Heffernan, Jr., "Political Activity and Social Work Executives," *Social Work* 9 (1964): 18–23.

18. For examples, see Patti and Resnick, "Changing the Agency from Within"; Daniel Thursz, "Social Action as a Professional Responsibility," *Social Work* 11 (1966): 12–21.

19. Briar, in *Social Work Practice*, pp. 26–27.

20. *Ibid.*, pp. 28–29.

21. See Briar (*ibid.*) for a discussion of the need for strong support from professional organizations for the social worker who acts as advocate. See also Wineman and James for a related discussion of this kind of institutional support, in the context of the social work student who is protesting dehumanizing practices in the social agency. David Wineman and Adrienne James, "The Advocacy Challenge to Schools of Social Work," *Social Work* 14 (1969): 23–32.

22. Howard and Somers maintain that the advocacy stance of the person in an agency in which dehumanizing practices occur can be a very satisfying means of combining resistance with participation in the system. Howard and Somers, "Resisting Institutional Evil."

23. John and Elaine Cumming, "Social Equilibrium and Social Change in the Large Mental Hospital," in Zald, *Social Welfare Institutions*.

24. David Daniels and John Kuldau, "Marginal Man, The Tether of Tradition and Intentional Social System Therapy," *Community Mental Health Journal* 3 (1967): 13–20.

25. Robert Rosenthal and Lenore Jacobson, *Pygmalion in the Classroom* (New York: Holt, Rinehart and Winston, 1968).

26. Earl C. Brennen, "The Casework Relationship: Excerpts from a Heretic's Notebook," *New Perspectives* 1 (1967): 65–67.

27. See, for example, Maxine Bucklow, "A New Role for the Work Group," *Administrative Science Quarterly* 11 (1966): 59–78; Dorwin Cartwright, "Achieving Change in People," in *The Planning of Change,* eds. Warren Bennis, Kenneth Benne, Robert Chin (New York: Holt, Rinehart and Winston, 1961); Eugene Litwak, "Models of Bureaucracy Which Permit Conflict," *American Journal of Sociology* 57 (1961): 177–84.

28. Rein's complete statement is even more to the point. He writes: "The principle of accountability to the consumer departs from traditional professionalism, which has been colleague-oriented rather than client-oriented." Martin Rein, "Social Work in Search of a Radical Profession." *Social work* 15 (1970): 13–28.

29. Howard and Somers, "Resisting Institutional Evil."

30. Weissman observed that the coalition of union workers and organized recipients in New York enabled the caseworker to do a better job and the clients to receive better service. Harold Weissman, *Community Development in the Mobilization for Youth Experience* (New York: Association Press, 1969), p. 105.

31. Bernard and Booth emphasize the tendencies of such alliances to come undone. Bernard and Booth, in *Can Public Welfare Keep Pace?*

32. Mechanic describes, in the context of other organizations, how a knowledge of the rules can be exploited, sometimes to support employees' contention that some rules can, in fact, be ignored. Citing Gouldner's study of mineworkers, he writes that rules can also be declared illegitimate and thereby ignored, when their observance would involve danger to workers. Mechanic, "Sources of Power," p. 364.

33. Howard and Somers, "Resisting Institutional Evil."

34. *Ibid.*

35. David J. Vail, *Dehumanization and the Institutional Career* (Springfield, Illinois: Charles C. Thomas, 1966).

36. Strategies that place staff members in some jeopardy, or others involving some question of ethics, have thus not been included, but this question has been addressed by others. See Howard and Somers' typology of "resister" roles. Howard and Somers, "Resisting Institutional Evil." Also see Patti and Resnick's statement about "marginally ethical" behavior: "Whether one uses marginally ethical means seems to us to rest on this assessment of the gravity of the problems or situations to be changed. Given organizational policies or practices that do serious harm to the well-being of clients or staff, we are inclined to agree with Alinsky that 'the most unethical of all means is the non-use of any means.'" Patti and Resnick, "Changing the Agency from Within," p. 57.

37. Wiener, "Social Change"; Thursz, "Social Action."

CHAPTER 8: HUMANIZING OTHER INSTITUTIONS

1. Vail's example of administration-initiated change to less dehumanizing practices is an indication that thrusts toward humanization can come from above as well. David Vail, *Dehumanization and the Institutional Career* (Springfield, Illinois: Charles C. Thomas, 1966).

2. Alvin Schorr, "Why Enforced Work Won't Work in Welfare," *Saturday Review*, June 19, 1971, pp. 17–19, 60–61.

3. Bernard Beck, "Welfare as a Moral Category," *Social Problems* 14 (1967): 258–65: William Ryan, *Blaming the Victim* (New York: Pantheon, 1971).

4. Marie Haug and Marvin Sussman, "Professional Autonomy and the Revolt of the Client," *Social Problems* 17 (1969): 153.

5. Eliot Freidson, *Profession of Medicine* (New York: Dodd, Mead and Co., 1970).

6. Robert Seaver, "The Dilemma of Citizen Participation," in *Citizen Participation in Urban Development*, ed. Hans Spiegel (Washington, D.C.: NTL Institute for Applied Behavioral Science, 1968), p. 67.

7. Morris Janowitz, *Institution Building in Urban Education* (New York: Russell Sage, 1969), p. 103.

8. Freidson chronicles medicine's long struggle to release itself from nonprofessional direction and comments that the milestone of being so released is a hallmark of a profession. Freidson, *Profession of Medicine.*

9. Haug and Sussman, "Professional Autonomy," pp. 156–57.

10. Herbert J. Gans, *The Urban Villagers* (Glencoe, Illinois: The Free Press, 1962).

11. Harvey L. Smith, "Crisis in an Institutional Network: Community Health Care," in *Institutions and the Person* eds. Howard S. Becker, et al. (Chicago: Aldine Publishing Co., 1968), p. 158.

12. Freidson, *Profession of Medicine*, p. 247.

13. *Ibid.*, p. 273. See also Ryan, *Blaming the Victim*, for related discussions.

14. As a further comment on the impact of societal forces, Sykes, commenting on a work program for inmates, states that the prison officials find themselves in the "uncomfortable position of needing the labor of their captives far more than do the captives themselves. . . . It is true that the prison will not go out of business, but the custodians may very well find themselves replaced." Gresham M. Sykes, "The Regime of the Custodians," in *Social Welfare Institutions*, ed. Mayer Zald. (New York: John Wiley and Sons, 1965), p. 441.

15. Elliott A. Krause, "Functions of a Bureaucratic Ideology: 'Citizen Participation,' " *Social Problems* 16 (1968): 129–43.

16. Terming this the "critical flaw" in professional autonomy, Freidson maintains that the profession develops a "self-deceiving view of the objec-

tivity and reliability of its knowledge and of the virtue of its members."
Freidson, *Profession of Medicine,* p. 369. He adds: "With the best of intentions [the profession] cannot see itself clearly and since its status protects it from others it cannot be seen clearly by them either. . . . It is the
special status that is the villain." *Ibid.,* p. 381.

17. Haug and Sussman, "Professional Autonomy," p. 156.

18. Janowitz, *Institution Building,* pp. 36–37.

19. Freidson, *Profession of Medicine,* p. 388.

20. Haug and Sussman, "Professional Autonomy," p. 158.

21. Whyte questions the inappropriate use of models in understanding
the therapeutic community. He suggests the labor relations model is a
truer reflection of power inequities than that of the community democ-
racy. William F. Whyte, "Models for Building and Changing Organizations," *Human Organization* 26 (1967): 22–31. For a discussion of the
power factor in service organizations see also Melvin Tumin, "Captives,
Consensus and Conflict: Implications for New Roles in Social Change," in
Social Theory and Social Invention, ed. Herman Stein (Cleveland: Press
of Case Western Reserve, 1968).

22. Sykes, "Regime of the Custodians"; Donald Cressey, "Contradictory
Directives in Complex Organizations: The Case of the Prison," *Administrative Science Quarterly* 4 (1959): 1–19.

23. Janowitz, *Institution Building,* p. 105.

24. Howard S. Becker, "The Teacher in the Authority System of the
Public School," in *Complex Organizations,* ed. Amitai Etzioni (New York:
Holt, Rinehart and Winston, 1965), p. 251.

25. Freidson, *Profession of Medicine.*

26. For a careful analysis of the falsity of this charge, see Ryan, *Blaming the Victim.*

27. As in welfare law, court cases have exposed the violations of civil
rights of tenants in government housing and there is much the same control over personal lives via admissions and evictions. Public housing direc-
tors have been likened to plantation bosses. See Jesse Grey, et al., "The
New Voices," *Public Welfare* 28 (1970): 14. See also Deutscher's discussion
of one aspect of that control. Irwin Deutscher, "The Gatekeeper in Public
Housing," in *Among the People,* by Irwin Deutscher and Elizabeth
Thompson (New York: Basic Books, 1968).

28. Ryan's major thesis in *Blaming the Victim* reflects this general defi-
nitional process. Even in institutions touching primarily upon middle-
class citizens, as Gouldner's discussion of red tape implies, clients are
viewed as untrustworthy, faceless, lacking rights to privacy and to the exercise of power. Alvin Gouldner, "Red Tape as a Social Problem," in
Reader in Bureaucracy, eds. Robert Merton, et al. (Glencoe, Illinois: Free
Press, 1952).

29. Howard S. Becker, *The Outsiders* (Glencoe, Illinois: The Free Press, 1963).

30. Robert Vinter, "Analysis of Treatment Organizations," *Social Work* 8 (1963): 12.

31. Neil Gilbert, *Constituents or Clients* (San Francisco: Jossey-Boss, Inc., 1970).

32. Besides wresting local control in some instances, organized parents can effect significant administrative changes, as witness the forcing of the New York school system to abandon the use of I. Q. tests. Gideon Sjoberg, et al., "Bureaucracy and the Lower Class," *Sociology and Social Research* 50 (1966): 325–37. See also Glazer for a comparison of this type of activity by the lower class with that of the middle class flight to the suburbs in order to have some mastery over more manageable institutions. Nathan Glazer, "White, Black and Community Control as the Issue," *The New York Times Magazine,* April 27, 1969.

33. John Ehrlich and John Tropman, "The Politcs of Participation: Student Power," *Social Work* 14 (1969): 65.

34. Smith, "Crisis in an Institutional Network," p. 162.

35. Students of some organizations, particularly in the correctional field, have commented on the existence of the bind, even short of clients' protests and the staff's adaptations to it. See, for example, Lloyd Ohlin, et al., "Major Dilemmas of the Social Worker in Probation and Parole," in Zald, *Social Welfare Institutions;* Cressey, "Contradictory Directives." Sykes describes this well: "Somehow [the prison administrator] must resolve the claims that the prison must exact vengeance, erect a specter to terrify the actual or potential deviant, isolate the known offender from the free community, and effect a change in the personality of his captives so that they gladly follow the dictates of the law—and in addition maintain order with his society of prisoners and see that they are employed in useful work." Sykes, "Regime of the Custodians," p. 431.

36. Harold Weissman, *Community Development in the Mobilization for Youth Experience* (New York: Association Press, 1961), p. 140.

37. David Daniels and John Kuldau, "Marginal Man, The Tether of Traditions and Intentional Social System Therapy," *Community Mental Health Journal* 3 (1967): 13–20.

38. Ohlin, et al., "Social Worker in Probation and Parole."

CHAPTER 9: CONCLUSIONS

1. Richard Cloward and Richard Elman, "Social Justice for the Poor," in *Poverty in America,* eds. Louis Ferman, et al. (Ann Arbor: University of Michigan Press, 1965), p. 330.

2. Phillipe Nonet, *Administrative Justice* (New York: Russell Sage Foundation, 1969), p. 91.

3. This limited consideration of income maintenance proposals is not meant to gloss over the many other elements involved in the several plans, but rather to extract those factors common to all which seem applicable here. For fuller discussions, see Eveline Burns, "Childhood Poverty and the Children's Allowance," in *Children's Allowances and the Economic Welfare of Children* (New York: Citizen's Committee for Children, 1968); Christopher Green, "The Negative Income Tax," in Ferman, et al., *Poverty in America;* Robert Lampman, "End and Means in War on Poverty," in *Poverty Amid Affluence,* ed. Leo Fishman (New Haven: Yale University Press, 1966); James C. Vadakin, *Children, Poverty and Family Allowances* (New York: Basic Books, 1968); Robert Harris, "Selecting a System of Income Maintenance for the Nation," *Social Work* 14 (1969): 5–13; Alanson S. Wilcox, "Patterns of Social Legislation: Reflections on the Welfare State," *Journal of Public Law* 6 (1957): 3–24.

4. See, for example, Robert Dahl and Charles Lindblom, *Politics, Economics and Welfare* (New York: Harper and Bros., 1953), pp. 154 ff.

5. Heather Ross, "An Experimental Study of the Negative Income Tax," *Child Welfare* 49 (1970): 562–69.

6. *Report of the National Advisory Commission on Civil Dosorders* (New York: E. P. Dutton; paperback edition: Bantam Books, 1968), p. 460.

7. Harry Jones, "The Rule of Law and the Welfare State," *Columbia Law Review* 58 (1958): 152.

8. Bernice Madison, "Canadian Family Allowances," *Journal of Marriage and Family Living* 26 (1964): 136–40; R. H. Parkinson, "Ten Years of Family Allowances," *Canadian Welfare* 31 (1955): 195–200; James Vadakin, *Family Allowances* (Miami: University of Miami Press, 1958).

9. Charles Reich, "The New Property," *Yale Law Journal* 73 (1964): 732–87. For a comparable sociological view of the stake the public has developed in the increased service functions of government see Morris Janowitz et al., "Public Administration and the Public," in *Complex Organizations,* ed. Amitai Etzioni (New York: Holt, Rinehart and Winston, 1965).

10. Jan Howard and Robert Somers, "Resisting Institutional Evil from Within," paper read at the Conference on Legitimation of Evil, San Francisco, 1970.

APPENDIX: ON METHOD

1. Phillip E. Hammond, ed., *Sociologists at Work* (New York: Basic Books, 1964).

2. This research is reported in Scott Briar, "Welfare from Below," *Law of the Poor,* ed. Jacobus ten Broek (San Francisco: Chandler Publishing Co., 1966).

3. Howard S. Becker, "Whose Side Are You On?" *Social Problems* 14 (1967): 239–47; Alvin Gouldner, "The Sociologist as Partisan: Sociology and the Welfare State," *American Sociologist* 3 (1968): 103–16.

4. Gouldner, "Sociologist as Partisan, p. 111.

5. Elliot Liebow, *Tally's Corner* (Boston: Little, Brown and Co., 1967), p. 13.

6. William F. Whyte, *Street Corner Society* (Chicago: University of Chicago Press, 1955), p. 320. My experience would also tend to confirm Whyte's view about research: "Logic plays an important part. But I am convinced that the actual evolution of research ideas does not take place in accord with the formal statements we read on research methods. The ideas grow up in part out of our immersion in the data and out of the whole process of living." *Ibid.,* p. 280.

7. Herbert Blumer, "Sociological Analysis and the Variable," *American Sociological Review* 21 (1956): 683–89; Herbert Blumer, "What Is Wrong with Social Theory," *American Sociological Review* 19 (1954): 3–10.

8. Richardson comments: "In any organization the leaders have a considerable degree of control over everyone within its framework. They have little or no control over research workers and may fear that they will disrupt relationships within the organization. [Also] they are not . . . familiar with many events that may be going on within their organization and they may not want research workers to find out things they themselves do not know." Stephen A. Richardson, "A Framework for Reporting Field-Relations Experiences," in *Human Organization Research,* eds. Richard N. Adams and Jack J. Preiss (Homewood, Illinois: The Dorsey Press, Inc., 1960), p. 135.

9. I found later that I had often paraphrased Blum's comments: "What I am writing," he said to staff members of an industry under study, "is a condensation and unification of all the stories you and your fellow workers tell me." Fred H. Blum, "Getting Individuals to Give Information to the Outsider," *Journal of Social Issues* 8 (1952): 36.

10. Melville Dalton, "Preconceptions and Methods in 'Men Who Manage,' " in Hammond, *Sociologists at Work,* p. 75.

11. For discussion of the balancing effects of a combination of individual and group discussions, see Howard S. Becker, "Problems of Inference and Proof in Participant Observation," *American Sociological Review* 23 (1958): 652–60. Agency limitations did not permit the luxury of both, except in a few unplanned instances. Also the discussion by Dean and Whyte about the "real beliefs" of informants is relevant both here and in relation to contradictions noted above. "It is assumed that there is invariably some basic underlying attitude or opinion that a person is firmly

committed to . . . his *real* belief. And it implies that if we can just develop shrewd enough interviewing techniques, we can make him 'spill the beans' and reveal what his basic attitude really is. . . . In fact, the conflict among these various subjective data may be the most important subjective information we can obtain." John P. Dean and William F. Whyte, "How Do We Know if Informant Is Telling the Truth," *Human Organization* 17 (1958): 35.

12. See Riessman for good discussion of the impact of the personality of the observer on the research situation and Dexter for a related discussion encompassing the effect of the observer's group affiliation. David Riessman and Jeanne Watson, "The Sociability Project: A Chronicle of Frustration and Achievement," in Hammond, *Sociologists at Work;* Lewis Dexter, "Role Relationships and Conceptions of Neutrality in Interviewing," *American Journal of Sociology* 62 (1956: 154–55.

13. For a discussion of the inevitability of this, see Peter Blau, *The Dynamics of Bureaucracy* (Chicago: University of Chicago Press, 1955).

14. Anselm Strauss et al., *Psychiatric Ideologies and Institutions* (Glencoe, Illinois: Free Press, 1964), p. 36.

15. Barney Glaser and Anselm Strauss, *Discovery of Grounded Theory* (Chicago: Aldine Publishing Company, 1967), chapter 5.

16. *Ibid.,* p. 106. The authors' method of analysis, in conjunction with the open plan of theoretical sampling, calls for continual coding of the data while new data are being collected. In fact, the purpose of theoretical sampling in their scheme is the search for new data as categories are being developed. This research plan varied since the data were in before the decision was made to use the constant comparative method of analysis.

17. Selznick is writing here of the TVA, but there is a distinct parallel here. Phillip Selznick, *TVA and the Grass Roots* (New York: Harper and Row, 1966), p. 249.

Index